MW01485830

UMAR IBN AL-KHATTAB
EXEMPLARY OF TRUTH AND JUSTICE

ARIF ULU

TUGHRA
BOOKS

New Jersey

Copyright © 2018 by Tughra Books

Originally published in Turkish as *Hakkın ve Adaletin Timsali Hazreti Ömer* in 2007.

21 20 19 18   3 4 5 6

Published by Tughra Books
345 Clifton Ave., Clifton,
NJ, 07011, USA

www.tughrabooks.com

Library of Congress Cataloging-in-Publication Data available

ISBN: 978-1-59784-281-5

Translated by Jülide Payette

Printed in Canada

TABLE OF CONTENTS

UMAR IN THE FOOTSTEPS OF HIS FATHER

Days and months went by. The son of Khattab was growing so fast. He was much stronger and taller than his peers. Khattab really liked his son's strength. Khattab took Umar wherever he went and had him wrestle with the other children, even with those who were older than Umar. Umar defeated the others, and his father, boasting highly about his son, told anyone that it was his child.

Khattab was doing his best so that his son would follow in his footsteps. Just like himself, he wanted his son to be a herdsman for their own animals. Thinking that someone like his son of great strength would be best suited for this job, he felt proud of his son, who was stronger than his peers. Because he knew that in order to be a herdsman in the mountains, one needed to be strong enough to cope with all the dangers.

Khattab taught Umar both this job and how to build an idol of *halva*[1] and of the other foods. He also taught Umar how to worship the same idols. He always recommended to his son that he bear respect for the idols, and in case of any need, ask the same idols for help. This was more than a recommendation; he took Umar with him to worship the idols.

Umar, thus, acted in compliance with his father's sayings. On the one hand, he was learning how to be a herdsman; on the other hand, he was building idols just like his father. Then he would stand before these idols and pray. If he felt hungry, he would even eat any one of these!

As a son and a father, they would go together to put the animals out to pasture. On one of those days, while letting the animals out of the barn, Umar turned to his father and said: "You don't need to come with me! I can do this by myself."

---

[1] A sweet prepared with sesame oil, various cereals, and syrup or honey.

Khattab really liked these words. He felt so proud of his son for presenting such an offer while his peers were engrossed in playing outside. From then on, it was Umar that put the animals out to pasture by himself. Yet, being a herdsman did not satisfy him since Umar, apart from being a strong and sound boy, was an intelligent child.

AN INTELLIGENT AND
A CAPABLE ONE

U mar grew and came to be a young boy who was strong and intelligent. He succeeded in everything, and as a young boy, he became a man of great distinction. In the years to come, he started to get involved with trade apart from being a herdsman. Thanks to his intelligence, quick-wittedness, and reliability and integrity, he attained great success in trade as well. As he grew older, he placed much more emphasis on trade and often traded with the caravans headed towards Syria.

Umar was one of the few people in his community who were literate. He was also competent in literature and poetry of pre-Islamic paganism. One can see this in his statement: "I can read a thousand couplet of poetry from the Period of Ignorance." Likewise, among his characteristics, he was a perfect orator.

Just because of his prominent characteristics, Umar was also given the responsibility of a messenger. Yes, it was he who was sent as a messenger and people would believe in his each and every word and act in accordance with the information he brought to them. Contrary to his young age, he played an active role in settling disputes between the tribes; often his decisions were eventually put into practice by the tribes.

VIOLENCE DURING THE
PRE-ISLAMIC PERIOD

U mar, in the footsteps of his father, was strictly committed to the traditions of the pre-Islamic paganism. Unfortunately, some of those traditions were very horrible and upsetting, the worst of which was the attitude towards girls. Men during those times would regard having a girl as humiliating and would make fun of those had baby girls. For this reason, those who had a girl would either kill them by burying them alive or would not pay any attention to the words of the ignorant.

Days went by. Umar got married and had three children, one of whom was a girl and the other two boys. Since Umar was quite devoted to the traditions of those times, he considered being the father of a girl humiliating. While he played and spent time with his sons, he did not even let his daughter sit on his lap and never kissed her.

His daughter grew up and turned five. Her getting older was not something good for Umar and made Umar enter into deep thoughts. It was because he was expected to kill that little girl before she got much older.

And that unfortunate day came. Upon awaking, Umar was much angrier than ever. He turned to his wife pointing at his little daughter, "Prepare her," he said.

He didn't even utter her name. His wife knew very well what would happen next. She burst into tears and looked at Umar. Her eyes were begging him to stop. She would not dare speak any word with Umar when he was that angry. Yet Umar did not pay any attention to her. Since he made his decision, it had to be on that day. He had never taken a step back in his life so far. His wife wept while she dressed her daughter.

Umar and the girl following behind her father passed by their house and headed towards the desert. A time later, people saw Umar coming back to town alone, pickax in his hand, and understood that he buried his girl.

Apart from this behavior of his which was far from merciful Umar, who was strictly committed to the other traditions of his time, would become angry when he saw someone who didn't behave properly towards the idols and attack that person. That state of anger, which no one dared to stop, even frightened his own relatives.

Yet, in spite of all these happenings, there were some people who were not covered with the dirt of that time of great ignorance. These distinguished people, very few in number, felt badly because of all of that was happening at that time, but there was nothing they could do to put an end to these traditions. It was the last Prophet who was the last hope of these very few people, who also knew very well the Holy Books, mainly the Bible and the Old Testament.

NOW IT IS TIME
TO CALL PEOPLE TO ISLAM

On the one hand, Umar and people very much like him were implementing the traditions of the Period of Ignorance they lived in. On the other hand, the fact that Prophet Muhammad, peace and blessings be upon him, was calling people to a new religion was heard by many in Mecca. God Almighty conveyed His religion to His distinguished Messenger, and told him to invite people to Islam beginning with people who were close to him. The very first supporters of the Messenger of God were his wife, Khadija who was his biggest confidant, his devoted friends Abu Bakr and Ali, who was very young, and his slave, Zayd.

Later, Uthman, Abdurrahman, Sa'd, Zubayr, and Talha, may God be pleased with them, were among those who were honored with Islam. Now it was the time for secretly inviting people to Islam. Calling to Islam was restricted to a small group of people who were made efforts for this end, but the number of people who believed the Messenger of God was increasing one by one. New verses of the Qur'an were being conveyed to him, and he shared these with Muslims around him. To this end, they mostly came together in quiet places, and it was the house of the Prophet that was generally used for these talks. In this way, the negative reaction of the Quraysh tribe was somehow avoided.

The polytheists, who were defying God with the idols that were built again by them, did not like these occurrences at all. They did not want to leave behind the beliefs of their ancestors to adopt the oneness of God and Muhammad, peace and blessings be upon him, as the Prophet. For the first years of Islam, they preferred to be just onlookers of the developments concerning the newly emerged religion. The polytheists simply made fun of whatever they heard in this respect and denied the Messenger of God as they thought that all these would come to a stop one day. Contrary to their expectations, this was not the case. With time, community members turned to the right religion one by one and became enlightened with faith.

Among those honored with Islam were some of the close relatives of the Messenger of God. However, none of his four uncles decided to follow him. Abu Talib did not oppose his sons, Jafar and Ali adopting Islam, but he did not renounce the religion of his forerunners. Although his uncles, Abbas and Hamza liked the Messenger of God very much, they could not decide whether to choose Islam as a religion or not. Unlike them, Abu Lahab explicitly accused his nephew of dishonesty, claiming that by turning away from the religion of their ancestors, they were making a very big mistake.

During this time of hidden invitation to Islam, the number of those that converted to Islam was not more than thirty. Believers worshipped in their houses and secretly read the latest verses of the Qur'an. Moreover, they met outside Mecca in quiet places to perform prayer in congregation.

When the verse *"(O Messenger) warn your nearest kinsfolk"* (Ash-Shuara, 26:214) was sent to the Messenger of God during the fourth year of his Prophethood, he gathered his relatives and made a big call to Islam.

Right then and there, Safiya, one of the aunts of God's Messenger, without any doubt, uttered her belief in God. Yet, the other aunts were not able to decide on it, but acted gently. At this time, Abu Lahab, one of the uncles of him, uttered these unpleasant words:

"O sons of Abdul Muttalib! This is a sheer wickedness, I swear! Stop him before others stop him." At that moment, Safiya opposed Abu Lahab:

"O my brother! Is it appropriate for you to despise and hold in contempt your nephew and his religion? Since scholars informed us that there would come a Prophet from the family of Abdul Muttalib, what is it with you then? How can you act this way?"

Abu Lahab continued his ugly speech in spite of his sister, and this time it was Abu Talib who, getting angry with Abu Lahab, said:

"O you coward! I swear to God that we will help and protect him as long as we live."

Turning to the Messenger of God, he said: "O son of my brother! I will be with you anytime. I will always protect you. You, go on inviting people to Islam."

Thus, they left that place.

In the coming days, the Messenger of God continued his call. While some people insisted on denying him and Islam, others complied with his calling and became enlightened with the faith. The Messenger of God climbed to the Hill Safa upon receiving the verse from the Angel Gabriel:

> So from now on, proclaim what you are commanded to convey openly and in an emphatic manner, and do not care (whatever) those who associate partners with God (say and do). We suffice you against all those who mock. (Al-Hijr, 15:94–95).

God's Messenger loudly proclaimed: "O people of the Quraysh!" When people heard his voice, they came and asked in wonder:

"O Muhammad! What has happened?"

In response, the Messenger of God said:

"If I were to inform you that enemy warriors are about to fall upon you from behind that hill, would you believe me?"

They all said:

"Yes! We would believe in you! We know you never lie and you are the one of great honesty."

God's Messenger heard what he wanted to hear. Afterwards, he said, "O sons of Fihr! O sons of Abdul Muttalib!" He then uttered one by one the name of all the families of the Quraysh tribe and said:

"My mission is to warn you. Come and protect yourself from the fire of hell. I invite you to say 'God is unique and there is no deity but God' and to come to faith. Unless you profess "*La ilaha illallah,*"[2] I can help you neither in this world nor in the next world."

It was only a few seconds after that Abu Lahab took a stone and shouted, "Shame on you! Did you gather us just to say this?" Then, he threw that stone towards him.

God's Messenger, however, continued:

---

[2]   There is no deity but God.

"O Quraysh tribe! Save yourselves from the punishment of hell! I have nothing to protect you from the punishment of God!"

That day there was not anyone other than Abu Lahab who reacted in this way.

None of them accepted what was said at that moment. They just talked among themselves and scattered. Upon the rejection and enmity of Abu Lahab, the *surah* al-Masad that begins with "*May both hands of Abu Lahab be ruined, and ruined are they!*" (Al-Masad, 111:1) was sent by God.

After this explicit invitation to Islam at Safa Hill, everyone in Mecca had heard about Islam. After inviting the sons of Abdul Muttalib to God, Prophet Muhammad, peace and blessings be upon him, started to gradually extend his chain of invitation to Islam. From this point on, he went to the Ka'ba without hiding, performed prayers there, called people to Islam, and explicitly read the Qur'an. Just like the Prophets before him, he said:

"O my tribe! Come and be only the slave of God Who has no equal."

The Meccan polytheists, who were living in darkness and ignorance, and who had no intention to stop believing in idols, at first turned a deaf ear to the invitation to Islam. However, with time, some of them showed an explicit enmity towards Islam. The unbelievers realized that with Islam, which commands people to stop their wrongdoings and misbehaviors, they would be rather restricted. Therefore, their anger and enmity towards God's Messenger grew more and more. In the meantime, the hajj season was coming. Arabs from all around Arabia were coming to Mecca and would hear about the invitation of the Messenger of God. This time, polytheists from the Quraysh started to contemplate how they would act upon facing such a condition.

They thought that most of the Arabs coming to Mecca in hajj time, after hearing the latest news there, would not come back to Mecca. This would, in turn, both negatively affect their trade business and impair their image and the respect towards the Meccans. Even worse, there was a possibility that the Arabs would all come together and remove the people of Quraysh from the Ka'ba. This would mean a Mecca that would be controlled by a different tribe. This was quite serious for them. It is for this reason that the unbelievers immediately came together and formed a consultative committee and started to talk about what they could do about this situation.

As a result of their talks, they decided to give the pilgrims and traders the message that the Messenger of God did not represent the people of Quraysh. The easiest way to do this was to tell everyone that he was not the Prophet. Some of them found it also necessary to call him mad while others decided to describe him as soothsayer, poet, or magician. Walid ibn al-Mughira, however, said that he had common points with the magicians although he was not a magician. In fact, all of them knew very well that Muhammad, peace and blessings be upon him, the most reliable one, was neither poet nor a magician. They even confessed this fact among themselves, yet they did not stop rejecting him and insisting on being ignorant.

In the end, the polytheists of the Quraysh decided to wait at the entrance points of Mecca and to warn those coming for the hajj. Preventing them from meeting with the Messenger of God, they intended tell them that there was a man named Muhammad who brought a new religion and totally disregarded all the idols. Thus, they intended halt the invitation of the Messenger of God. He, ignoring all of this, continued to inform people about the revelations of God.

THE NIGHT AT THE KA'BA

The beloved Prophet was, on the one hand, coping with all those troubles during the day, but at night he went to Ka'ba when everybody was deep asleep and performed prayers and supplications there. The Ka'ba was of big importance not only to the Messenger of God, but also to Umar, the son of Khattab. He went to the Ka'ba almost every day, cleaned his idols, and bowed in front of them in full respect. He even stayed in Ka'ba until the next day. In one of those days, he came to Ka'ba toward the evening. The Messenger of God was also there. As usual, he started to read the Qur'an. He was reciting the *surah* al-Haqqah.

Umar heard the voice of the Messenger of God. Having a perfect knowledge of Arabic literature and able to read thousands of couplets of poem by heart, Umar was startled upon hearing the Qur'an being read by God's Messenger. Because what he heard was in no way similar to the poems he had learned from those important poets. Both his heart and mind was heavily influenced by the recitation. However, he told himself, "I should not be influenced." He thought that he would be able to convince himself that he was a poet just as the Quraysh had called him. In this way, he thought, he could persuade both his mind and heart and feel relief. "Yes, he is a poet, he said to himself."

While he was challenging himself in this way, God's Messenger went on reciting the *surah* Al-Haqqah. Right that moment, he was reading these verses:

> It surely is the speech (conveyed to you by) an illustrious, noble Messenger, and not a poet's speech (composed in a poet's mind). How little is what you believe! (It is so limited by the poverty of your souls and hearts). (Al-Haqqah, 69:40–41).

The verses recited by the Messenger of God were a perfect answer for Umar, and he was rather startled. He was given the answer for the questions he wondered in himself. Yet, he could not stop the voices in his heart and mind. If he also called him a soothsayer as the other idolaters did, he thought he would be able to convince both his mind and heart. "Yes, he is a soothsayer," he said.

While Umar was having this struggle in himself, the Messenger of God continued to recite the *surah*. At that moment, the he recited the verse: "*Nor is it a soothsayer's speech (pretending to foretell events). How little it is that you reflect and be mindful! (It is so limited by the poverty of your minds).*" (Al-Haqqah, 69:42).

Umar, immediately again, found the answer to his questions. It was the answer that criticized him for not contemplating and challenging his mind. The Messenger of God went on reciting the Qur'an while Umar listened in surprise. He finished reciting the *surah*. However, the thoughts of Umar did not come to an end. Umar was heavily influenced by what he had heard. In order to get rid of the effect of the words, Umar immediately left that place.

The verses of the Qur'an were on his mind. He did not believe the claim that God's Messenger was a poet or a soothsayer because he knew very well that what he had listened to that night belonged neither to poets nor to the soothsayers. He was unable to sleep that night. During the whole night, he suffered from the attack of ideas, and in this way the morning arrived. However, the son of Khattab, Umar, could not change his old stance. He could not take the step that would provide him with salvation. He could not stop believing in the idols that he believed in since his childhood. As he did always, he stood up and directly went to his idolater friends. Joining them, Umar forgot whatever he lived the day before. Even though he came so close to the truth, he was dragged into the darkness of the unbelief again.

THE FIRST SANCTUARY AGAINST TYRANNY: ARQAM'S HOUSE

The polytheists, failing in the prevention of the spread of Islam despite their oppression, more increased their tyranny against the Muslims. Wherever they saw Muslims, they attacked them and tried to beat them to death. They heavily tortured especially those who did not belong to any tribe. It was not possible to call them human considering all this violence. They tortured the Yasir family, who did not give up their religion, to such an extent that both Yasir and his wife Sumayya were killed. Even this did not stop the hatred of those unbelievers. They made Ammar, the son of Yasir family, lie on the sand glowing with sun wearing an iron shirt thereby "melting his bone marrow".

The unbelievers also tortured the Messenger of God. They were always insulting him and throwing the dirty paunch of a camel at his pure body. In the face of all this torture, the only thing he did was to turn to his Creator and say, "My God, I am leaving the Quraysh to You."

God's Messenger and his friends had no desire other than worshipping God. However, they could not worship in the Ka'ba which was built in the name of God as a result of the obstructions imposed by the unbelievers. Trying to avoid the evil actions of the people in Mecca, the Messenger of God did not allow his Companions to worship at the Ka'ba. As a result of the talks with his friends, he decided to gather in a certain house so that they could be protected from the tyranny of the unbelievers. This house, which would provide him and his Companions with a safe place to worship, was the house of Arqam in the narrow street west of the Safa Hill. Upon this decision, God's Messenger and his friends started to secretly come together at the house of Arqam. They learned by heart the verses of the Qur'an sent by God and prayed there.

GO ANYWHERE IN THE UNIVERSE

I t had been five years since the mission of calling people to Islam was assigned to the Messenger of God. He and his friends went on worshipping in the house of Arqam and secretly inviting the non-believers to Islam. The fact that people believing in God were exposed to unbearable tyranny made the Messenger of God quite sad. The rage of the unbelievers was not likely to fade away either.

During these days of big troubles and difficulties, God showed a way out for His Messenger through Gabriel:

> Say (quoting Me): "O My servants who believe: keep from disobedience to your Lord, in reverence for Him and piety. For those devoted to doing good in this

world, aware that God is seeing them, there is good (by way of recompense). And God's earth is vast (enabling worship). Those who are patient (persevering in adversity, worshipping God, and refraining from sins) will surely be given their reward without measure. (Az-Zumar, 39:10).

With this verse of the Qur'an, God recommended that the Muslims migrate. As a result, the Messenger of God gathered his friends at the house of Arqam and told them:

"Go anywhere in the world; God will bring you together again."

Then, his Companions asked:

"O Messenger of God, where shall we go?"

He pointed towards Ethiopia and said:

"It would be good to go towards Ethiopia. It is a safe place. There is a ruler there, in whose country nobody faces tyranny."

Complying with the Messenger of God, his Companions immediately started preparing for their journey. A group of fifteen people said farewell to God's Messenger and set off. Those migrating were able to worship God in peace in Ethiopia. This was what they wanted. They left the place where they grew up so that they could put into practice their religion. Thanks to this migration, both the Muslims were able to escape from the oppression and the neighboring countries heard about Islam.

DIRTY PLAN

The unbelievers were closely watching the Muslims migrating to Ethiopia. They wanted to cause them trouble even in those faraway places. They started to plan on how to expel the immigrant Muslims from Ethiopia. In their struggle to persuade Muslims to leave Islam, the believers were shocked by the news that Hamza, who was famous for his courage and heroism, also joined the group of the Messenger of God. The unbelievers heard this news very rapidly. As a result, they came together to make some decisions towards the prevention of Islam. One of the indispensable names, Umar was also at the meeting, one of many they had organized in order to stop Islam.

He was sitting next to Abu Jahl, one of the eternal enemies of Islam.

One of the participants started to speak:

"We certainly have to take some precautions. Those among the most powerful of the Quraysh have started to join him."

Another participant said in anger:

"Hamza joined him, too. If we do not act immediately, I cannot even imagine how far that will spread."

Those newly learning that Hamza also joined Islam could not conceal their surprise. Looking at each other, they said:

"Hamza? We would never expect him to do such a thing."

One of the famous people of Mecca uttered:

"Yes, friends! As it is clear from what you said, there is only one thing to do. We have to eradicate the problem before it gets much more complicated."

Some of the participants could not exactly understand what he meant. When asked how they would be able to solve the problem, that person just explained his dirty idea in this way:

"The only thing we can do is to kill Muhammad!"

Another one just said:

"Yes, you are right. None of the cautions we have taken so far have worked. The number of those believing in him is increasing day by day. There is no any other way to stop all this to kill Muhammad."

The unbelievers decided to kill the Seal of the Prophets. But who was going to do this? And how? They began to debate over who would kill him. It was not easy to kill the one who came from the sons of Hashim and towards whom the love increases more and more. One of the participants spoke:

"OK, but who will kill him?"

In the meantime, looking at around in anger, one of them saw Umar, the son of Khattab. It was well known that Umar had been among those who most harshly reacted against the Messenger of God in those days when he began to explain his mission and invite people into Islam. He just said to himself: "Yes, I have found him." He needed to say this. Without asking permission to speak he shouted:

"I know the one who will kill him."

All of them stood in silence, waiting to hear the name that would be uttered. The man cried.

"It is Umar!"

Those knowing Umar all agreed that it was the right name.

They all started talking among themselves:

"Why didn't we think about it before?"

Yes, Umar was the most appropriate person for them as well. He was both powerful and totally against the newly emerged religion. Someone who was not that furious against the religion, even if he had been powerful, would not have dared kill one of the sons of Hashim.

All the eyes there turned to him. Umar, keeping his silence so far, spoke in rage:

"Yes, I can do this at any cost. I can do anything to kill the one who is against our idols."

Those participating in the meeting went on talking. Yet Umar had no patience to listen to them. He thought that he could not wait even a minute in vain since he undertook such an important mission. All of a sudden, he stood up and said:

"I am going."

Later, he added with his strong voice:

"I will find and kill him!" he yelled.

All of the people there were waiting in silence and watching Umar. They stood up altogether to see him off. They were all in joy. The most serious problem they faced would be solved in such an easy way. They thought that Umar would succeed in it because "with this rage and power, Umar would not let Muhammad live."

Taking his sword, Umar slammed the door and headed for the place where God's Messenger was.

UMAR'S SURPRISING JOURNEY

Upon Umar's leaving, people there did not scatter. They wanted to enjoy that moment. They thought they would be able solve such a big problem thanks to the rage of Umar. He, sword in his hand, was headed for his target. He could not bear even the idea that the number of those accepting the newly emerged religion was rapidly increasing, and he burst into anger. He began running towards his target, saying, "I know what to do with you." While he was talking to himself on the road, he ran into a man. It was Nuaym, who was one of Companions hiding the fact that he accepted Islam. Seeing Umar in rush, Nuaym called out to him:

"Why are you in such a rush, Umar? Where are you going?"

Umar, taking a harsh look at Nuaym, responded:

"To kill Muhammad!"

"Why?" asked Nuaym.

"He declares himself as a Prophet and people believe and join him. With his words, he influences people to abandon our idols. Besides, their number is so rapidly increasing, we have to eradicate this problem so that we can find peace," said Umar.

Nuaym was startled by Umar's words. He really loved the Messenger of God and would not bear the idea that something bad would happen to him. He felt he had to talk to Umar and stop him. However, Umar was so angry and decisive that it was not possible to persuade him to stop. Then he thought he should gain some time. So, he said:

If you kill Muhammad, his tribe, the sons of Hashim would find you and kill you.

The words of Nuaym had no effect on Umar because he had already taken all of this into account. What Nuaym was trying to do was to save time so that he could inform God's Messenger about this. Therefore, he told Umar:

"I heard that your sister and her husband joined them and became Muslims. I think you should first stop them before Muhammad."

Umar could not believe his ears.

"No, I do not believe you. You are making this up," he yelled.

When Nuaym said:

"Then, if you do not believe me, you should first go to your sister's home and ask them."

Umar's answer was this:

"OK. I am going. But if what you told me was not correct, you will pay for it."

Then, he left. He changed his route and decided to go to the house of his sister, Fatima and her husband. Walking so fast, he could not stop himself from thinking, "If these allegations are true…" What would his friends say if they heard about this?

In the meantime, without losing any time, Nuaym arrived at Arqam's house. At that moment, God's Messenger was talking with his Companions. Nuaym told the Messenger *of God* word for word what he had heard on his way.

Umar, on the other hand, was walking so rapidly, because of anger, he couldn't see even those passing by him. In the end, he reached the house of his sister and her husband. He heard voices coming from the house. At the house were his sister, Fatima, her husband Said ibn Amr and Habbab, one of the Companions. Right at that time, Habbab was reading the verses of the Qur'an saying: "*Assuredly, it is I. I am God; there is no deity save Me. So worship Me, and establish the Prayer in conformity with its conditions for remembrance of Me.*" (Ta-Ha, 20:14). Umar tried to understand what these voices were saying.

He got close to the window, and now he could hear the voices much better. What he heard made Umar recall the night at the Ka'ba. He started to be influenced again, yet his anger prevented him from thinking properly.

He got closer to the door and began knocking harshly at it. Those at the house understood that it was Umar. Habbab, in a second, concealed himself somewhere in the house. His sister and her husband wanted to hide the pages on which the verses of the Qur'an were written. Because they knew that if Umar saw them, he would go mad. Very worried, Fatima said:

"We have to hide these right now. If Umar sees these, he will get angry with us."

They put the pages of the Qur'an in a secret place. The voices were no longer audible. Umar was by now banging at the door and shouting:

"It is Umar. Open the door."

The sister of Umar, Fatima, opened the door in great fear. Umar quickly moved toward his sister's husband. He asked him:

"Did you change your religion? Have you joined the religion Muhammad brought?"

Understanding that Umar had heard him reading the Qur'an, his sister's husband said:

"Maybe the religion we chose is better than yours."

This time Umar became furious. He jumped over his sister's husband and started to kick him. His sister, upon such an attack, tried to intervene to stop Umar. Umar slapped his sister too and made her face bleed. Bleeding, Fatima stood up and decisively said:

"Look Umar, it is not right to believe in idols as you do. The true faith is what the Prophet brought us from God Almighty."

Seeing the determination of his sister and her husband, Umar understood that he could not force them to give up their religion despite all his efforts. At that moment, those interesting words he had heard came to mind. Turning to Fatima, he said:

"Show me what you were reading."

His sister and her husband looked at each other. Fatima said hesitantly:

"We fear that you will harm them."

"Don't worry. I will not do anything to the pages."

Upon his answer, Fatima brought back out the pages of the Qur'an. Umar, after performing the ritual ablution of the whole body in the way his sister explained, took the pages. There was written *surah* Ta-Ha. Umar started to read that *surah*, after which he became calm and felt peace in his heart. Then turning to his sister and her husband, he said:

"These words belong neither to a poem nor to a human being."

His sister and her husband found it too difficult to believe their ears. Umar got calmer and calmer. He started to calmly read the pages. After finishing reading, he said:

"Take me to Muhammad."

The husband of his sister, bewildered, uttered these words:

"Why do you want to go him? Are you planning to harm him?"

Upon this, Umar said:

"I was craving to kill him until I came here. But when I read the pages you showed me, I wanted to hear what he teaches."

Watching all of this happening from the place he was hiding, Habbab became very excited when he heard the words of Umar. He appeared all of a sudden. Seeing him, Umar was bewildered because he had not known that Habbab was also at the house. He had heard that Habbab had accepted Islam. Thinking that he could learn something about the Messenger of God and the religion to which he invited people, Umar said:

"Talk to me about Muhammad and the religion he brought.

Habbab started to speak. Umar was heavily influenced by Habbab's explanations and confirmed the accuracy of what was told to him. All of a sudden, he stopped and looked at Habbab:

"I want to join and accept your religion, too. Take me to Muhammad."

Habbab was overjoyed. Turning to Umar, he said:

"O Umar! Right now, you have found the right way. I believe that you have the blessing of the Messenger of God."

At once majestic Umar fell to his knees. What he felt when he was coming to this house was totally different than what he was feeling now. He had been angry, yet that anger was now replaced by peace. All he wanted was to go to the Messenger of God as soon as possible. Turning to Habbab again he said:

"O Habbab! Take me to him."

Habbab in a big joy and excitement replied:

"OK. Let's go right now."

Umar and Habbab together set off. They headed for Arqam's house. When they got closer to the house, the Companions saw that Umar was coming. Those witnessing all the violence Umar had imposed upon Muslims were rather concerned. They feared that he would harm the Messenger of God. Right away, they went to God's Messenger and asked him what they should do. He said in a quiet, calm manner:

"Let him come here."

"All right, O Messenger of God," they said but in rather a concerned manner.

"But what if Umar had an ill intension," they thought.

Hamza, who was well-known for his heroism, said:

"Do not worry. What good news if Umar is good-intentioned. If not, I will kill him with his own sword."

Upon these words of Hamza, the door was opened. Habbab together with Umar entered. They said: "Peace be with you." Umar directly went towards the Messenger of God, sat in front of him, and said that he wanted to be Muslim. Later, together with the Messenger of God he said:

"I bear witness that there is no deity but Allah, and I bear witness that Muhammad is His Messenger.[3]

---

[3] Islamic confession of faith.

The Companions were so happy with this that they all together started saying: "*Allahu Akbar! Allahu Akbar!*"[4] Since Umar was one of the most powerful, courageous, and smartest ones at that time, they thought that Umar's being Muslim would add to the power of the Muslims.

The way that led Umar to kill the Messenger of God suddenly turned into the one that put him at the source of enlightenment. God accepted the prayers of His Messenger. He had prayed in this way: "O God! Strengthen Islam either with Umar or Amr ibn Hisham (Abu Jahl), with the one who is more lovable before You." Umar, may God be pleased with him, accepted Islam thanks to the prayers of God's Messenger and because God bestowed him with such a blessing.

Following Umar's becoming a Muslim, God's Messenger named Umar "Faruq," which means the person who can see the difference between right and wrong, between darkness and enlightenment. From that day on, Umar was also called Faruq.

---

[4] God is the All-Great.

LEAVE FROM ARQAM'S HOUSE

U mar was also at the house of Arqam. The number of the Muslims had reached forty. With the other Companions, Umar sat right in front of the Messenger of God and listened to him in humility. Not wanting to hide this change in himself and craving to explain it to all of Mecca, Umar asked him:

"O Messenger of God! Are not we responsible for calling people to Islam whatever it costs us?"

"Yes, I swear to God that you are in charge of inviting people to Islam whatever it costs you," he said.

Getting this answer, Umar asked:

"Then what is the meaning of hiding in this house? We should go out and invite people to Islam."

Umar had another wish. He wanted to pray at the Ka'ba where he really liked to sit and pray. For the last days, the Messenger of God had not allowed his friends to stay and pray there to keep them safe from the dangers coming from the idol worshipers of Mecca. For this reason, they worshipped together at Arqam's house. Seeing this big desire in Umar, the Messenger of God welcomed his wish. They went out of Arqam's house; in the front was God's Messenger, at his right was Umar, at his left was Hamza followed by other Muslims. Chanting "*Allahu Akbar*," they headed towards the Ka'ba. As soon as they arrived at the Ka'ba, they thanked God and prostrated. They had really missed the Ka'ba.

There were many people there at that time. Umar was both walking around the Ka'ba and loudly repeating the Islamic confession of faith. The whole Ka'ba was echoing with loud voice of Umar. Those seeing this scene right away went to Abu Jahl and told him:

"Muhammad is now much stronger. Umar has joined them too."

Abu Jahl found it too hard to believe this since he had heard that Umar intended to kill him just a few hours ago. Turning to them, he asked:

"Where did you hear this?"

They responded:

"If you do not believe us, go and see it for yourself at the Ka'ba."

Abu Jahl, in a big hurry, stood up and went directly to the Ka'ba. In the meantime, Umar just left the Ka'ba, and was coming to Abu Jahl. Coming closer to Umar, he said:

"They say that you have changed your religion. Is this true?"

Umar, in rather a confident manner, said:

"Yes, what you have heard is right. I think that there is not anyone or anything other than God to worship, and I accept the fact that Muhammad is His Messenger."

Upon hearing this, Abu Jahl and his friends went mad. It was because of the fact that a very influential person, preferring God's Messenger, had left them and added to the power of him. It also meant that killing the Messenger of God was not possible anymore. A group of idol worshipers from Mecca, not accepting the fact that Umar had left them and became Muslim, attempted to attack Umar. The conflict between them lasted a long time. At that time Al-As ibn Wail, one of the prominent names of Mecca, was at the Ka'ba. Seeing that people of the Quraysh tribe were fighting with Umar ibn Khattab, who was from the Adiyy tribe, he said to them:

"O people of Quraysh! What are you doing?"

When the people of Quraysh said:

"Umar collaborated with our enemy. Now he is repeating what he has learned from Muhammad in front of us." Al-As ibn Wail put an end to the fight, saying:

"Let Umar go. He has chosen his own way. What do you want with him? Can you imagine that people within the Adiyy tribe will leave such an important man amongst themselves at the hands of you?"

Thus, following his victory over his very own self, Umar performed his first struggle.

It was not an ordinary case that Umar accepted Islam. Abdullah ibn Masud, one of the important names among the Companions, talked about the importance of the fact that Umar chose Islam in this way: "Umar's becoming Muslim is a conquest." Umar came to be a perfect person when his intelligence, courage, and power combined with Islam. It was very soon that he came to be one of the closest friends of the Messenger of God.

EMBARGO

The increase in the number of Muslims and the fact that important names in Mecca such as Hamza and Umar had accepted Islam were driving idol worshipers crazy. Polytheists came together and made a new decision. This decision included clauses that would deprive Muslims of their rights to live. Polytheists wrote their decisions on papers and attached them on the walls of the Ka'ba. These decisions said that until the Messenger of God was delivered to them — dead or alive — both the relatives of God's Messenger and Muslims would be declared enemies. Nobody would have, in any way, contact with Muslim people. Nobody would marry any one of these people, trade with them, and they would not even speak with them. In compliance with this decision, the unbelievers subjected the Muslims to economic and social isolation. The polytheists put into practice those decisions one by one. They did not allow people to talk to the Muslims and did not trade with them in the markets. Hence, the Muslims came to be deprived of basic things; they were unable to feed themselves.

This embargo lasted exactly three years. Relatives and Companions of the Prophet Muhammad, peace and blessings be upon him, did not leave him at the hands of the polytheists. In the end, the polytheists gave in, and the relatives of the Prophet tore apart the agreement hanging on the wall of Ka'ba and put an end to the embargo.

THE SACRED JOURNEY BEGINS

All the plans made by the unbelievers with the purpose of preventing the spread of Islam were in vain. Their applications for the embargo did not work either. What's more, thanks to this, Islam spread in the region, and the hands of the Muslims strengthened.

As it was usual, in the eleventh year of Islam during the hajj time, Mecca was filled with Arabs coming from all around. God's Messenger, as usual, went to invite the visitors coming to Mecca to faith. On one of those days, he saw on the Aqaba Hill, which stood between Mecca and Mina, six people coming from Medina. He recited the Qur'an for them and called them to Islam. Right after listening to him, these six people from Khazraj tribe in Medina accepted

Islam. Thus, they became the first people from Medina to enter Islam. They told the Messenger of God that they would come here again during the next hajj season and then left. When they returned to their home, they started to explain Islam to other people. A year later, during the hajj season again, once more six people came with the former six people, and they met the Messenger of God. Each one of these twelve people pledged their allegiance to the Prophet. After this, he designated these twelve people as responsible for the tribes there. The polytheists were able to learn this only after everything happened because the Muslims came to the meeting place secretly and separately. Therefore, they could not do anything to stop this.

With the last Aqaba allegiance, Medina came to be a safe and comfortable place for the Muslims. As a consequence of the torture and the pressure inflicted by the polytheists upon the Muslims, the Muslims could barely find any place to sustain their lives. Because of this, they were allowed by God to migrate to Medina. As a result, in the fourth year of the Prophethood, the Muslim people began to leave Mecca in small groups.

Thus began a new process. Lovers of God who had no desire other than saying: "My Creator is Allah, Muhammad is His servant and Prophet" got permission from the Prophet Muhammad and left their beloved hometown. They went to faraway places and migrated to Medina. They took enough food with them to sustain them only for a few days. All of their houses and belongings remained in Mecca.

The news of the Muslims' emigration to Medina spread quickly in Mecca. The polytheists, fearing that Islam would rapidly spread in Medina, sought ways to prevent Muslims from going to Medina. They did their best in order to catch those who were migrating. It was for this reason that Muslims went out in groups only in the middle of the night when all people went to sleep.

One day, Umar came to the Messenger of God and asked for permission to migrate. Just like the other Muslims migrating, he would also go to Medina with his friends. Umar, Ayyash ibn Abu Rabia, and Hisham ibn As agreed to

migrate together. The three friends came together and reviewed their plans for the journey.
They agreed to meet at the outskirts of Mecca very early the next morning. Umar and his
friends all knew that the unbelievers of Mecca
were doing their best in order to prevent Muslims from migrating. Thus, they agreed that "if
one of us does not arrive there at the time we all
agreed, we will know that this friend has been
stopped by people from Mecca, and the others
will not wait for that friend but continue on
their journey."

They set off without knowing what that journey would bring them. Umar thought that he
would not set off without paying a visit to the
Ka'ba which had become very dear to him after
accepting Islam. He could not stand the idea of
not seeing the Ka'ba for a long time. After leaving his friends, Umar put on his sword, took several arrows and directly went to the Ka'ba. All
prominent members of the Quraysh were sitting
in a circle in the courtyard of the Ka'ba. Umar
first circumambulated the Ka'ba seven times,
prayed there, and then coming to the place
where the polytheists were sitting, he shouted:

"Yes, I am going, too. Not because I am afraid of you, but because the Messenger of God wants me to do so. If there is anyone who can dare to see his mother's suffering from the loss of his son, to see his children orphaned and his wife widowed, I will find that person behind that valley."

The unbelievers of Mecca knew very well how powerful and angry Umar was. They knew that Umar had wrestled even with camels in his childhood. For this reason, nobody dared to speak.

Upon leaving the Ka'ba, Umar prepared for migration. It was such a sad migration as neither his wife nor his children went with him. He was all alone on that hard journey. This was the only way he was able to migrate anyway.

He got up very early in the morning and performed his prayers. Then he said farewell to his family. He headed for the place where he would meet with his friends. When he arrived at the meeting place, he saw Ayyash. He had just arrived. Apart from Ayyash, twenty Muslims joined them. These Muslim people knew that if they migrated with Umar, the unbelievers of Mecca would not be able to harm them.

It was only Hisham who did not arrive at the meeting point. Thinking that he would come soon, they waited. Yet Hisham did not come. Thinking that Hisham was stopped by the un-believers of Mecca, they left with Ayyash. They were right. Hisham was imprisoned and stopped from migrating by the polytheists of Mecca. Al-though Umar had told the unbelievers of Mecca the route he would follow, none of them dared to come and stop them. The unbelievers saw that among those Muslims migrating was Ayyash. They could not dare to stop him since he was with Umar and informed Abu Jahl and Harith ibn Hisham about the situation as Ayyash, Abu Jahl, and Harith ibn Hisham were relatives on their mother's side and cousins.

HALF OF MY WEALTH IS YOURS

Following a difficult journey, Umar and Ayyash arrived in Quba, a place quite close to the Ka'ba. There they stayed with the tribe of Amr ibn Awf. In the meantime, Abu Jahl and Harith had already started to follow Ayyash. They rode their camels as fast as possible. They wanted to prevent their relative Ayyash, from migrating to Medina. The reason they wanted to do so was not that Ayyash was related to them but because they wanted to make people believe that "Friends of Muhammad are leaving him." They wanted to realize their aims as soon as possible. In that hurry, they arrived in Quba very soon. They found Umar and Ayyash and tried to speak to them. Umar knew very well both Abu Jahl and Hisham. He understood their intentions at the first moment he saw them. Umar said to himself:

"They could not have come here with good intentions. They came here to set a trap for Ayyash."

Yes, Umar was right in his assumption. Abu Jahl and Harith, acting sad on the surface, turned to Ayyash and told him:

"Your mother was very upset upon your leaving. She vowed not to comb her hair nor seek shelter from the sun."

Abu Jahl knew very well that Ayyash loved his mother so much and was deeply committed to her. He thought that he could prevent Ayyash from this path only through such lies. Upon hearing this, Ayyash went pale and his voice started to tremble.

Seeing the mood of Ayyash, Umar thought that he could be easily deceived. Looking at Ayyash, he said:

"I swear to God, what they intend is to divert you from your religion! They are lying. Be cautious! If your mother wishes, she will comb her hair and protect herself from the sun of Mecca."

Abu Jahl reached his aim. Ayyash voice went on trembling. Turning to Umar, he said:

"I shall go, talk to my mother, and please her. I have some belongings there, too. I shall take them with me."

Umar understood that Ayyash was very inclined to go. Without any hesitation, he presented Ayyash with a big offer:

"You know very well that I am one of the richest among the Quraysh. I shall give you half of my wealth. But no way can you go with them."

Umar was insistent on not letting Ayyash return to Mecca because he experienced the beauty and the bounty of Islam. He could not bear even the idea that one of his friends would return to those ignorant days, the pre-Islamic paganism. He was ready to give half of his wealth that everyone envied without any hesitation.

Umar felt he knew what would happen to Ayyash. He knew what a sly unbeliever Abu Jahl was. Still, Umar could not persuade Ayyash not to go. Ayyash could not understand the real purpose of those coming to him, so he decided to go with them. Umar did not want to lose his friend. Again turning to him, he said:

"OK. You are insistent on going. Then take my camel. May camel is both a fast and docile one. Sit on it and never get off the camel. If you feel someone deceiving you, it will help rescue you."

With the permission of Umar, Ayyash set off together with Abu Jahl and Harith. Abu Jahl and Harith did not tell Ayyash anything before leaving Quba. They knew that if Ayyash heard their real intentions, Ayyash would leave them right away. Unfortunately, Ayyash did not understand their ill intentions."

Umar and his friends arrived in Medina. Muslims from Medina and the immigrants coming from Mecca met Umar and other twenty Muslim people with great joy.

As for Ayyash, he went to Mecca with Abu Jahl and Harith. He was quite confused. On the one hand, he felt bad that he gave up the migration. On the other hand, he was happy because he would please his mother. In an effort to mitigate his sadness, he told himself: "I will persuade my mother and return."

While he was engrossed in such confusion, Abu Jahl and Harith both agreed that it was time to act on their ill intentions. Turning to Ayyash, Abu Jahl told him:

"My friend, my camel is exhausted. Yours goes very fast. Can I use yours for a while?"

Ayyash had to make his camel kneel and sit so that Abu Jahl could take a seat. Not understanding the conspiracy, Ayyash said:

"Of course, I will make my camel kneel and sit, then you have a seat."

Ayyash had already forgotten Umar's saying: "In no way make your camel kneel and sit, never dismount from your camel." He made his camel kneel and Abu Jahl sat on it. They continued on their journey. Abu Jahl, without losing any time, started to put into practice his malicious plan. He tied Ayyash's hands. At that time, Harith stopped his camel and approached them. They quickly made Ayyash dismount from the horse. Ayyash could not understand what was happening. In this way, they made him enter Mecca. Abu Jahl went on implementing his malicious plan. Taking Ayyash to a place full of people, Abu Jahl addressed the people of Mecca:

"O people of Mecca! We have brought back our relative from Muhammad. You also bring your own relatives who were deceived by the sayings of him and never leave them again!"

It was only now that Ayyash understood the conspiracy.

Ayyash, under the control of Abu Jahl, directly went to his mother. It was too late, but he saw that whatever was said by Abu Jahl and Harith were not correct; what they intended was to divert him from Islam. He sought ways to turn back to Medina. However, he was taken under custody by both Abu Jahl and other unbelievers of Mecca.

Umar was rather concerned upon Ayyash's leave. But he could do nothing either. If Abu Jahl tried to take Ayyash by force, he would not have let this happen. It was for this reason that Abu Jahl and Harith had constructed such a plan. They could not dare to take someone by force in the presence of Umar. It was Ayyash who was convinced to return to Mecca because of his mother. Umar, who was so self-sacrificing that he would have given half of his wealth so that one more person was enlightened with Islam, could do nothing but allow him to leave.

DAYS IN MEDINA

After the Migration, Umar's life in Medina began. He was happy because he acted in compliance with the orders of God and His Messenger. Yet he was feeling upset in the very depths of himself. He was apart from the Messenger of God, the person whom he loved most and from whom he could not part for even a minute. Since accepting Islam, he had never been that far away from God's Messenger. He was craving for the day he would be able to see him again. One day he heard that the Messenger of God set off with Abu Bakr to migrate, and he felt a big joy. Umar was the happiest man at that moment.

The news the Messenger of God had left Mecca with his loyal friend Abu Bakr for Medina travelled fast in Medina. The city was filled with a great joy. People of Medina went out every day and waited for them to come. Finally, the day they were waiting for came. Upon hearing that God's Messenger and his Companion were so close to Medina, people lined up on the road leading to Medina. All people—mothers, fathers, grandmothers, grandfathers, and children were all there. Everyone was waiting for them in great excitement and joy. Umar was there, too. The Messenger of God for whom he had waited for many days was finally coming. He was very happy. The children of Medina were also delighted. They would see God's Messenger whose name they heard all the time but whom they had never seen before.

One of them said:

"Here they come."

Right that moment, their excitement doubled.

Altogether they started to yell:

"Yes, they are coming."

The children were full of joy and focused on the people coming. It was the time on which they waited for so long. The pride of humankind was coming to Medina.

The Messenger of God said to the people waiting for him impatiently: "Peace be with you." The people of Medina told the guests:

"O our distinguished guests, welcome all of you! Medina is honored by you. It is good that you came."

Later, they hugged each other. Umar hugged God's Messenger in such a way that all the people who saw them were highly affected by this scene. Everyone shouted in joy. From now on, the Muslims were much happier.

Umar's joy was difficult to describe. He was very happy because he was with the Messenger of God, whose side he could not leave even for a minute, and his loyal friend Abu Bakr.

However, Umar could not stop thinking about something. He was always thinking about Ayyash with whom he migrated. When the situation of Ayyash was explained to the Messenger of God, he was very upset too and prayed for him.

In the meantime, Ayyash was still under the control of Abu Jahl and Harith. One day, he received a letter from Umar. In the letter Umar told him:

"The Messenger of God was quite upset with your case and prayed a lot. I also would like to see you return to Medina."

He also attached some verses of the Qur'an to the letter. Reading the letter, Ayyash felt resentment. He wanted to be at that blessed place at once. When he learned that the Messenger of God had prayed for him, he burst into tears. His desire to go to Medina also increased then.

One night during the following days, he found the chance to secretly leave Mecca, and he headed for Medina. On the way, he thought about the self-sacrifice Umar had made for him, and at the same time he recalled the trick conceived by his brothers. The more he thought about the fact that the Messenger of God prayed for him, the faster he rode his camel. He arrived in Medina after a long journey. His loyal friend came to meet him. Umar, not considering his mistake, hugged him so closely. Altogether they went to the Messenger of God. Ayyash was very happy. Yet, Umar was perhaps happier than him because a friend of his had been rescued from returning to the traditions of pre-Islamic paganism.

BROTHERHOOD

The Muslims of Mecca were able to bring a few things with them during their migration to Medina. In the name of their belief, they left just about anything of themselves; their houses, belongings, date groves, vineyards, and orchards. As for the Muslims of Medina, they met their brothers of Mecca on the way and hosted them for days long. Even some of the Muslims of Medina whose houses were very small left their houses for their guests and found another place for themselves and their families to sleep.

The Muhajirun (Muslims migrating from Mecca) made great sacrifices for the sake of their faith and religion while the Ansar (Muslims helping the Muhajirun in Medina) who

welcomed and embraced them acted accord-
ingly, with an unequaled dimension of sacrifice.
Although the Muslims of Medina were poor, the
only source being farming, they embraced and
did their best to please their brothers of Mecca
with whom they shared the same religion.

The Ansar of Medina used any opportunity
at their hands for the Muhajirun coming from
Mecca. The fact that most of them found already difficulty in sustaining their lives made the
people of Mecca upset. The Ansar were always
decent and smiling at them, yet the people of
Mecca felt they were a big burden on the Ansar.
The Messenger of God, observing this situation
for a while, gathered the Ansar and Muhajirun
one day. He explained to them the situation
they were in and matched every family of Mecca with one of the Muslim families of Medina
and declared them as brothers. These brothers
would share their houses and jobs. They would
work together and share anything they earned.

The Ansar of Medina sacrificed greatly.
They willingly shared anything of themselves
with their brothers and sisters of Mecca. It was
such a big sharing that they somehow tried to

more please their brothers of religion than their own brothers. This was something that could not be understood by those who did not believe in God and His Messenger.

ONE DAY YOU, ONE DAY ME

G od's Messenger declared Umar and Utban ibn Malik as brothers. Utban was willingly sacrificed everything for his brother, Umar. This deeply affected Umar. Umar, who was adept at anything and could do anything in a perfect way, always helped Utban. They went to the date grove together, worked together, and returned to their houses together. Similarly, they trade between themselves, too. Umar shared his knowledge of trade coming from his childhood with Utban.

Umar and Utban were much closer to each other than the brothers who had blood ties. They talked, prayed, and went to the Messenger of God together. Now more people were coming to their house, and they had to work harder.

They spent a certain amount of their earnings for the other Muslims who were in need of help.

Yet, Umar was undergoing a problem in himself. Umar, who became a big lover of the Prophet since he first accepted religion before the Messenger of God, wanted to stay longer with him. It was not sufficient for him to perform prayer all day just behind him. He wanted to stay longer with him, to hear and learn any word coming from him.

At night, he could never go to sleep because of such deep thoughts. He told himself, "I must certainly explain this to Utban." He wanted to share this with his brother, who would do anything for Umar. One morning, he decided to talk to Utban about his desire to spend more time with the Messenger of God:

"Brother, we are going to God's Messenger, but this is not enough for me. I want to learn more from him. I want to know what he says when we are not with him."

Utban was not surprised at the wish of Umar. He also wanted to spend more time with the Messenger of God. Yet, they were both well aware of the fact that they needed to work. Ut-ban, turning to Umar proposed an idea:

"Perhaps you can go and listen to the Messenger of God on one day, and then I will go the next. The one that goes to listen to him shall share with the other whatever he has learned that day."

This offer pleased Umar, too. He thought he would not be able to hear the Messenger of God every day himself, yet he would learn his teachings anyway. There was no one happier than Umar at that moment. He would both help his brother who shared his house with Umar and his work and would not miss any of the teachings of God's Messenger.

SUCH A BIG CHANGE

Muslims were facing many problems in their new lives at Medina. The Messenger of God consulted with his Companions about their problems and solved most of these problems with Abu Bakr and Umar, his two closest friends. These two distinguished Companions were the closest confidants of the last Prophet. When the Messenger of God mentioned about them, he would say: "I have two viziers in the heavens, as for my viziers on earth, they are Abu Bakr and Umar."

Umar, thanks to the faith in his heart, improved greatly. Once Umar, who without any hesitation had said "Me!" upon being asked "Who will kill Muhammad?" now came to be the person who most consulted with the

Messenger of God on every issue. He abandoned anything material and strove for Islam regardless of his life and wealth. This state pleased the Messenger of God. When he spoke with the Companions about Umar, he would say: "There is no angel on earth that does not pay respect to Umar. There is no devil on earth that does not run away from Umar."

Because Umar pleased God as well, one day God Almighty ordered His Messenger to tell Umar that he would be granted Paradise. The Messenger of God told Umar this good news, and Umar felt extremely joyful and embraced the Messenger of God. Despite this good news, he never felt comfortable and certain about himself; he struggled for this holy goal until the last minute of his life.

UNBELIEVERS STILL DO NOT GIVE UP

M uslims had left their homeland and wealth at the hands of the unbelievers for the sake of living their religion and migrated to Medina. Therefore, they did not have a rich life in Medina, yet they were very happy since they could easily worship God. They established a new state here. They lived in peace with their neighbors. The people of Medina started to get to know the Muslims, and in groups they began to embrace Islam. Hearing this, the unbelievers were highly frustrated and raged. In order to intimidate and harm the Muslims, the polytheists attempted to attack the Muslims several times. Yet, upon learning the plans of the unbelievers, the Messenger of

God sent out units to fight against the unbelievers. The polytheists were defeated, and they again escaped to Mecca. Nevertheless, they never gave up disturbing the Muslims.

One day, the Companions saw the Messenger of God concerned and asked him the reason for this. He said that the unbelievers of Mecca were preparing a big army for a battle. The Messenger of God did not want to fight, yet they had to protect themselves anyway. Therefore, he also formed an army consisting of his Companions. The Muslim army was made up of 313 people. The unbelievers of Mecca set off with a huge army. They were rather confident about the power of their army. The Muslim army moved from Medina and established headquarters near the well of Badr.

Although they were ready, the Messenger of God was not a supporter of fighting, and so he sought alternative ways to end the conflict. In the end, they wanted to send a messenger to the unbelievers to say that they did not want to fight. It was Umar who had acted as the messenger during these dark days.

Assuming the task given by God's Messenger, Umar, without losing any time, went to the headquarters of the unbelievers. He sent them the message saying that, "There shall not be battle." Abu Jahl, the commander of the unbelievers made fun of Umar:

"It seems that Muhammad is afraid of us."

Later he added:

"We are here for the battle. We will never give up fighting."

Seeing this battle as a big opportunity to get rid of the Muslims, the unbelievers did not accept the peaceful suggestion of the Messenger of God.

Umar turned back and informed God's Messenger about the situation. There was nothing to do. The Prophet Muhammad, peace and blessings be upon him, gathered the Companions and asked their opinions on this matter. The Companions replied:

"We are ready."

Thus the fight that would be written in history as the Battle of Badr began. It lasted almost five hours. God granted help to the Muslims who coped with any difficulty for the sake of worshipping God. The Muslims, who were less in number compared to the unbelievers, defeated the unbelievers who were confident about the size of their army. Almost seventy unbelievers, among whom was Abu Jahl, were killed.

THE BATTLE OF UHUD

It was the year 625, and only one year had passed since the battle. The unbelievers could not accept the big defeat at the Battle of Badr. They all sought ways to avenge this defeat. They wanted to catch the Muslims unprepared for any attack. It was especially Hind, the wife of Abu Sufyan, who incited the unbelievers of Mecca for revenge since her father had been killed during the Battle of Badr.

One day, the people of Medina heard that the unbelievers were forming a more powerful army for a new war. The Messenger of God gathered the Companions and informed them about this news coming from Mecca. Although he did not want to fight, he began to prepare for defense and wanted his Companions to prepare as well.

Without losing any time, the Companions began preparations for the battle. Umar joined them. While the Muslims were getting prepared for the battle, they heard that the unbelievers of Mecca were perfectly equipped and getting closer to Medina with three thousand soldiers. It was Friday. The Messenger of God and his friends set off after Friday prayer. God's Messenger had a thousand soldiers with him. Yet, three hundred of these gave up fighting halfway and left the army. Those leaving the army came to be considered *munafiqun*. They were Muslims on the surface, but in reality they were not. Their purpose was to harm the Muslims. The Messenger of God and seven hundred soldiers went on their way. In the next morning, at the time of Morning Prayer, they got close to the Mountain Uhud.

The battle was about to start. The Messenger of God stationed fifty archers on the hill at their left and instructed them:

"Archers! Do not let the mounted unbelievers attack us from behind. Do not leave your places whether we lose or win the battle. Even if you see that we are all killed, do not leave your places."

Umar took his place on the front. The battle was on. It was very soon that the unbelievers lost many of their people as a result of the attacks of the Muslims. The Muslims were close to winning the battle. Some of the archers who were placed on the hill by the Messenger of God saw this victory and assumed that they won the war. Forgetting about the warning of not leaving their places under any circumstances, they left their station. The generals of the other side saw this and wanted to made use of the opportunity. Therefore, they besieged the Muslims from their back. The forgetfulness of the archers cost many lives. That day, almost seventy Muslims were killed, among whom was Hamza.

THE SOLUTION THAT
BEWILDERED THE UNBELIEVERS

I t had been two years since the Battle of Uhud
and six years since the Migration. The unbelievers of Mecca were making plans to completely eradicate the Muslims.

The unbelievers formed an army consisting of
exactly ten thousands soldiers in order to actual-
ize their evil plans over the Muslims. The Messenger of God gathered all the Companions of
Medina in the Masjid an-Nabawi (the Prophet's
Mosque) right away. They consulted with each
other on the course they would follow. Salman
al-Farisi, who was of Iranian origin, said:

"O Messenger of God! When we heard that
their soldiers were planning to raid, we dug dig

ditches around us to prevent them from getting close to us. We can do the same thing here, too."

Both God's Messenger and the Companions liked Salman's idea. Yet, they did not have much time for this. They had to dig those ditches in a month at maximum. All the Muslims mobilized for this purpose. Anyone who could work and even the children were digging ditches, and the Messenger of God helped them with all of his effort. While digging, the Companions encountered a big rock that they could not handle and came to the Prophet, saying:

"O Messenger of God! While we were digging ditches we ran into a big rock. We did our best but couldn't break it."

Upon this, the Messenger of God took the Salman's sledgehammer. The Companions followed him. He said *Bismillah* (In the Name of God) and hit the rock with that sledgehammer. One third of the rock was broken, and there appeared a big spark. Everyone stared at him in wonder.

The Messenger of God said:

"*Allahu Akbar!* The keys of Damascus have been just given to me. I swear by God that I see the red manors of Damascus."

He went on breaking the rock. Repeating *Bismillah*, he hit the rock a second time. There appeared again a big spark, and a part of the rock was split apart.

He said:

"*Allahu Akbar!* The keys of Persia have been given to me. I swear by God that I see the city of Madayin of the Chosroes and his white manors!"

He said *Bismillah* for the third time and hit the rock again. The rock was totally torn to pieces now, and there appeared a spark again. The Companions all turned to the Messenger of God and were waiting for the explanation of his.

He said:

"*Allahu Akbar!* The keys of Yemen have been given to me. I swear by God that I see the doors of the city of Sana'a."

All of the places that the Messenger of God uttered were eventually conquered during the caliphate period of Umar and Uthman, and the Companions, may God be pleased with them, saw their conquest.

After the hard work that lasted all day and night, the ditches were ready. The length of each ditch was almost five kilometers. As for its width, it would not allow a horse to pass to the other side of the ditch. If someone had fallen in it while trying to pass over the ditch, he would not have been able to get out of the ditch.

Not long after the completion of the ditches it was heard that the unbelievers of Mecca were getting closer to Medina with their ten thousands soldiers. The Messenger of God assigned certain tasks for the Muslim soldiers. He stationed each and every one of them in certain areas of the city.

Upon entering Medina, the unbelievers were in total surprise; they were face to face with something they had never seen before: the ditches. They could not understand what was happening. The ditches prevented them from setting foot in the city, yet they had no intention of turning back either because they had been preparing for this war for months. They surrounded the ditches. Even some, risking their lives, tried to jump over the ditches. Seeing this, the Messenger of God put the best fighters of His Companions in the most critical places. He placed Umar, who was quite adept at using sword, at a point where the unbelievers were most struggling to pass. The unbelievers incessantly attacked from the points

Umar was protecting. That day, a massive group made an attempt to pass from that point. Seeing that the unbelievers were many in number at that point, the Messenger of God sent reinforcement for Umar. Umar and the other Companions killed the soldiers of the unbelievers. Seeing this, the unbelievers immediately ran away from the point where Umar was standing.

Thus Umar drew back the unbelievers and put those trying to pass in the ditches. He became the exemplary of heroism, but he was a bit sad because he had missed his afternoon prayer during the battle. Umar came to the Messenger of God and explained his situation. He, revealing that he also was unable to perform prayer during the heated struggle, consoled Umar.

The unbelievers surrounded the ditches for exactly twenty-seven days. However, they were unable to enter the city. Those trying to enter into the city were killed by the Muslims. Believing that continued fighting would cause more losses for them, the unbelievers ended the siege and headed towards Mecca in frustration. With the help of God, the Prophet Muhammad, peace and blessings be upon him, and the Companions gained another big victory.

TENSION AT HUDAYBIYA

After the Battle of the Trench, the Messenger of God saw himself with his Companions circumambulating the Ka'ba in a dream. In the next day, he explained this dream to his friends, and then turning towards those who were looking in wonder he said: "We will circumambulate the Ka'ba."

He later wanted his Companions to get prepared for this. Immigrants of Mecca missed their hometown from which they had been away for six months for the sake of putting into practice the creeds of their religion. He told those who wanted to go for *umra* (minor pilgrimage) to get ready immediately. He, together with his one thousand and five hundred friends, was ready to go to Mecca. With the instruction of the

Messenger of God, they moved from Medina to
Mecca. Since the only thing they wanted was
to go for umra, they did not take any weapon.
The Messenger of God visited the grave of his
mother and prayed there. Then, they continued
their travels. They reached the Hudaybiya region. This region was almost a day away from
Mecca. They had been traveling for days. They
were exhausted. With the instruction of God's
Messenger, they decided to spend the night
there and pitched their tents.

The people of Mecca heard that the Messenger of God and one thousand and five hundred friends of his left Medina and were coming
towards Mecca. The unbelievers of Mecca were
in panic then. They tried to learn the purposes
of the Prophet Muhammad, peace and blessings
be upon him, and his Companions. They decided
not to let them into Mecca and immediately sent
a messenger among themselves to the Messenger
of God. The Messenger of God explained their intentions to the messenger, but the attitude of the
people of Mecca had not changed. God's Messenger wanted to reiterate to them that they had
no aim other than going for umra. Thus he sent

a messenger from among the Muslims to them, yet the unbelievers of Mecca were rather rude towards this messenger. They even attempted to kill him. The messenger barely escaped and returned to the Messenger of God. He, this time, wanted to send Umar. Umar, of course, wanted to perform the will of the Prophet, yet he had one concern. Turning to the Messenger of God, he said:

"The unbelievers are very angry with me. If I go there, their anger could grow. It would be much better to send Uthman."

He agreed with Umar. Bani Umayya, one of the prominent tribes of Mecca, were cousins of Uthman. The members of this tribe would not allow the unbelievers to hurt Uthman. What's more, Uthman was a calm person. The unbelievers did not bear the same hatred towards him as they did towards Umar. Therefore, the Messenger of God decided to send Uthman to Mecca instead of Umar. He asked that Uthman send the message that "Muslims are not coming here to fight, but for umra."

He had one more request from Uthman. There were some people who turned to Islam and had to hide this fact from the unbelievers.

Not forgetting them, the Messenger of God wanted Uthman to visit them and tell them that the conquest was very close, and soon they would not have to hide their faith anymore.

Uthman left right away for Mecca. He went to the unbelievers and told them everything one by one. Yet, it fell on deaf ears. The unbelievers yelled at him:

"Go and tell him that he will never be able to set a foot in Mecca and circumambulate the Ka'ba."

Later they added:

"If you want to circumambulate the Ka'ba alone, here you are, you can."

Uthman declined this offer by saying that:

"As long as the Messenger of God does not, I will not either."

These words of Uthman made the unbelievers very angry. They decided to imprison him. While Uthman was in custody, the Messenger of God and his friends all waited at Hudaybiya. Everyone was expecting Uthman to persuade the unbelievers and return with good news. However, time passed and Uthman still did not arrive. A question arose in all minds: "Did the unbelievers of Mecca do something bad to Uthman?"

This question preoccupied their minds. The Muslims caused a big loss for the unbelievers of Mecca in each of the three big battles. In order to take revenge, they may have decided to harm anyone who was close to the Messenger of God. The more they waited, the more concerned they became since Uthman had not yet returned. God's Messenger was rather concerned as well. Like his friends, he began to think that the unbelievers may have done something bad to Uthman. If they had harmed him in a peaceful time, when there was not any battle or other conflict, the Messenger of God would not let such an act go unpunished.

At some point, it was said that Uthman was killed by the unbelievers. The Messenger of God gathered his Companions and listened to them swear their allegiance that they would fight against the unbelievers and punish them, whatever the cost, and they would never leave him. This allegiance has been called the Pledge of Ridwan.

This allegiance the Messenger of God received from the Muslims really feared the unbelievers. They immediately sent messengers to the Messenger of God with Uthman and told that they wanted to make an agreement. Later, an agreement between the Muslims and the unbelievers of Mecca was signed. This agreement was named the Hudaybiya Agreement, and it included decisions such as:

"The Muslims and unbelievers will not battle for ten years. The Muslims will return without visiting Mecca that year. The visit will be paid in the next year, and it will last only three days. The Muslims will not bring any weapon except their swords, on condition that their swords remain in their scabbards. In case any Muslim from Medina returns to the unbelievers, these people will not be returned to the Muslims. However, if someone from Mecca joins those in Medina, they will be immediately returned to Mecca even if they are Muslims. Arabic tribes will be free to align themselves with either God's Messenger or the Quraysh."

The Companions who caused big losses for the unbelievers of Mecca in each of the three big battles found the clauses of this agreement quite disadvantageous. The clause that said any Muslim coming to the Messenger of God from Mecca during this period would be returned to the Quraysh made the Muslims almost crazy.

On the surface, the clauses of the agreement seemed totally disadvantageous for the Muslims. Yet, the Messenger of God knew very well what he had signed. The fruits of this agreement would be seen in the future, yet the vast majority of the Companions could not understand it at that time. Among these was Umar. He could not hide his anger when he heard the content of the agreement. Coming to the Messenger of God, he shouted with his resonant voice:

"Are you not the Messenger of God?"

In fact, Umar was very respectful towards the Prophet Muhammad, peace and blessings be upon him, despite his tough nature. He showed an utmost respect towards him and never raised his voice when he was with him. But when he learned the content of the Hudaybiya Agreement, he could not stop himself. The Messenger of God was still calm in the face of Umar's anger, and he answered his questions softly:

"Yes, I am the Messenger of God."

"Are not we, as Muslims, on the right path while the unbelievers, as our enemies, are on the wrong path?"

"Yes, we are on the right path. And the unbelievers are on the wrong path."

"Then, why do we accept that vileness? Why do we allow them to humiliate our religion?"

"I am the slave and the Messenger of God. I cannot act contrary to the commands of God. I did not rebel against God by accepting the clauses of this agreement."

"Did you not tell us that we would visit the Ka'ba?"

"Yes, I did. But I did not say it was this year. I say it again that you will certainly go to Mecca and circumambulate the Ka'ba."

The clauses of the agreement, especially the third one, turned Umar mad. He could not stop himself even after talking to the Messenger of God and directly went to Abu Bakr. He was still angry. He asked Abu Bakr the same questions:

"O Abu Bakr! Isn't Muhammad the Messenger of God?"

"Yes, of course. He is the Messenger of God."

Then, are we, as Muslims, doing the right thing while our enemies, the unbelievers, were doing the wrong thing?

"Yes, we are."

"Then, why do we allow them to humiliate our religion?"

"O Umar, Muhammad is the Messenger of God. He, by making this agreement, did not act in contrary to God. He is under the close watch of God. God helps and aids him. We have to obey him.

Umar went on with his questions:

"Then, didn't he tell us in Medina that we would go to Ka'ba and circumambulate it?"

"Of course, he did. But, did he say that we would go there this year?" Abu Bakr replied.

"No, he didn't."

"If he said 'We will visit the Ka'ba very soon,' then we will go to the Ka'ba and visit it very soon."

Unlike some Companions, Abu Bakr was calm and in the line with whatever was supposed to happen.

Indeed, he was Abu Bakr, as-Siddiq (the Truthful One). He was the most prominent of all truthful ones.

After the agreement in Hudaybiya, the Muslims headed towards Medina. Umar, later, realized that he had hurt the Messenger of God. The calmer he became, the better he understood this. He had not been able to control himself at that time. He began to ask himself, "How did I utter such words to the Messenger of God?"

God's Messenger was hurt. In fact, he knew this nature of Umar. Perhaps he did expect such a reaction from someone that was so close to him.

The more Umar thought, the better he understood the future benefits of the agreement signed. Anytime he remembered his attitude towards the Messenger of God, he was once more devastated. Whenever he thought about it, he felt totally embarrassed and that God would not forgive him since he made the Messenger of God sad.

Wishing for forgiveness, he fasted a lot, performed prayers, and even released some slaves. However, he could not get rid of the feeling of not being forgiven anyway because the Messenger of

God did not smile at him as he had before. With the purpose of apologizing to and making up with the Messenger of God, he approached him with a question, but he did not answer. A certain time later, he approached him again and reiterated his question. Again he could not get an answer from him. Soon, he wanted to try once again hoping that he would forgive him. This time, again, he got no response from the Messenger of God. That great Umar was in a total despair. What was he going to do if his Prophet, whom he could not stand not seeing even for a day, did not look at him again?

With these thoughts Umar rode his camel fast and passed in front of the crowd. He was getting angry with himself, saying "How could I do such a thing?" Like Umar, many other Muslims could not understand the Hudaybiya agreement. However, Hudaybiya played a very important role in the announcement of Islam. With this agreement, the unbelievers of Mecca officially recognized both the Messenger of God and the state of Islam. Besides, a year after this agreement, Muslims would be able to visit the Ka'ba with the utmost ease, and this event would be talked for days long. During this time, Khalid ibn Walid, Amr ibn al-As and some others, all of whom were prominent names of Mecca, would accept Islam by their own free will. Likewise, God described this agreement as a conquest and sent the *surah* al-Fath.

Umar, unaware of this *surah*, was in deep thought, heading towards Medina in the first rows of the crowd. A loud voice behind him called: "O son of Khattab!" Umar, in his deep thoughts, could not recognize the voice calling him. The same person called Umar again with a louder voice. This time Umar stopped his camel right away and waited for the one that addressed him. He was concerned. He thought perhaps he was going to be punished for his actions. In the meantime, the voice that called him came very close to Umar. He told Umar:

"God's Messenger is waiting for you."

At the moment Umar heard the name of the Messenger of God, he longed for him. Immediately, he turned back and directly went to the Prophet Muhammad, peace and blessings be upon him. Umar was both worried and excited. He was wondering why the Messenger of God had summoned him and what he was going to say. He was somehow relieved to see him because there was a smile on the face of the Messenger of God. Turning to Umar he said:

"O son of Khattab! God sent me a *surah*. With this *surah*, He informed that Hudaybiya was a victory," and then he read this *surah*.

Standing up, Umar hugged the Messenger of God and again apologized to him. He was the Prophet of mercy. He hugged Umar whom he loved much and forgave him. Now Umar was relieved. For the rest of the journey, he was with the Messenger of God, quite happy and peaceful.

God's Messenger knew each one of his Companions very well, and he was aware of this angry nature of Umar. It was something innate for Umar. Maybe it was for this reason that he was not that upset by the behavior of Umar. In fact, the Messenger of God knew that Umar's attitude in Hudaybiya was the reflection of his sincerity. It was Umar, leaving behind any blessings given in this world, preferred Islam regardless of the possibility of being hungry. Umar also drew lesson from this event.

After this event, the attitude of the Messenger of God towards Umar never changed. Umar was still one of his best friends with whom he consulted most.

When the very innate characteristics of Umar combined with Islam, he became a perfect person. With his intelligence, broad horizon, and other features bestowed by God, Umar hit the mark with his words and actions. During the period of the revelation of the Qur'an, some of the verses confirmed his ideas on certain subjects. It is called *tawafuqat* when an idea proposed by someone is in line with a verse of the Qur'an that has not been sent yet. According to some scholars, the verses of the Qur'an were in line with the views of Umar at least fifteen times, to some others twenty-one times. In relation to this situation of Umar, his son, Abdullah ibn Umar, said this:

"If, on a certain topic, my father proposed an idea and another proposed something different than that of my father, the verses of the Qur'an revealed later confirmed those of my father."

THE FIRST *WAQF*

I t had been a year since the Hudaybiya agreement. The Messenger of God arranged a battle against the people of Khaybar who collaborated with the unbelievers and betrayed the Muslims. The Muslims conquered Khaybar. In those periods, the wealth that was acquired as a result of the battles was distributed among those who joined the battles. The Messenger of God divided the lands that were taken as a result of the battle among the Companions. The Messenger of God allocated some valuable land for Umar as he did for the other Companions. Some Companions turned these lands into date groves, others into gardens.

As for Umar, he had no intention of doing either of them. He wanted to make use of this land in a different way. He liked and preferred to spend only the money he earned through his hard work. He lived on trade. He would give most of his earnings from his trade to the poor and spend them for the sake of God. He was very generous. Before Islam, he used to spend his money and wealth on the unbelievers; now he offered it only to his Muslim brothers.

He was always thinking about the land he acquired from Khaybar. What should he do with this piece of land? At last, he decided on how to make use of that land. He turned the land that was given to him into a *waqf* (endowment or foundation) and arranged a document listing the terms of the usage of this *waqf*: "This land shall not be sold, donated, or owned through inheritance. The income coming from it shall be spent for the poor, relatives, slaves, guests, and for those that act in the name of God."

Umar did not want this land to be connected to his name. He thought that if it was, he would unwillingly feel somehow a proud when he saw this land. Therefore, he wanted someone else to manage the property. The condition for the one who would control this land was as follows:

"The person who manages the *waqf* could reasonably use the yields himself and give them to other people." Thus, Umar showed his difference again and gave the land that was assigned to him to the poor. This land became the first *waqf* as such.

NO MORE HOMESICKNESS

I t had been eight years since the Muslims left their hometowns, their goods, and properties and migrated to Medina, and it had been two years since the Peace Treaty of Hudaybiya. The unbelievers of Mecca, as usual, were not keeping their promises. Although they signed the Hudaybiya agreement, they had begun to violate some clauses of the agreement. According to this agreement, if they wished, the tribes would be able to establish partnership either with the Messenger of God or with the people of the Quraysh.

While some tribes were collaborating with the unbelievers, the Huza'a tribe was at the side of the Muslims. The unbelievers could not accept this and were always disturbing the Huza'a tribe. One day, they attacked the Huza'a tribe and killed exactly twenty people. Thus, they violated the agreement. Before, it had not meant much for them to break an agreement. However, now they were aware of the fact that the Muslims were getting stronger and stronger. They knew that if they violated the agreement, this would put them in a more disadvantageous position. Therefore, they did not want to lose any time. They immediately sent Abu Sufyan to Medina to meet the Messenger of God. Abu Sufyan approached him and said:

"O Muhammad! We shall remake the Hudaybiya agreement and extend its duration."

God's Messenger asked:

"O Abu Sufyan! Did you come here to say this?"

"Yes, I did," he replied.

God's Messenger asked again:

"We have upheld the existing version of the agreement. Did you violate the agreement?"

The Messenger of God knew that the unbelievers had not acted in accordance with the agreement in recent times. By asking this question, he may have wanted Abu Sufyan to confirm this situation. Bowing his head to the ground, Abu Sufyan could not answer the question. A time later, with a hoarse voice, he said:

"No, we did not do such a thing. We want you to rearrange and lengthen the duration of the agreement."

The Messenger of God did not respond to his wish. In despair, he left him and directly went to Abu Bakr. He begged him to be a mediator in the rearrangement of this agreement. Abu Bakr did not accept his demand. When he was unable to get a positive response from Abu Bakr, Abu Sufyan went to Umar without losing any time. He begged Umar:

"O Umar! Help me. Tell Muhammad to rewrite the Hudaybiya agreement." Umar, angry with the unbelievers for what they had done against the Muslims, said:

"Then, you breached the agreement that you made with us? I will not say anything to the Messenger of God about rewriting this agreement. I will also fight against you on this issue as well."

Two closest friends of the God's Messenger did not support Abu Sufyan. However, he did not intend to give up, and it was because the Muslims had come to be much stronger. In the event that the Messenger of God and his friends initiated a war, the unbelievers would not have the power to fight anymore.

With the last hope, he went to Uthman, Ali, and other prominent Companions, may Allah be pleased with them. Yet, they all rejected his proposal. Therefore, he had to return to Mecca in failure. The people of Mecca waiting the return of Abu Sufyan saw him and asked:

"Did you persuade them? Are we going to make a new agreement?"

Abu Sufyan explained to them what had happened. Later he added:

"Unfortunately, I could not persuade them."

Fear in the people of Mecca then increased. They believed that the Messenger of God would punish them since they violated the agreement, and they could not foresee when this would happen.

The Messenger of God was intending to organize a battle against the unbelievers of Mecca who violated the agreement. Yet, he kept this idea to himself so that he could catch the unbelievers unprepared. He did not want bloodshed; he had hoped to retake Mecca without any battle. Anyway, he had always been against bloodshed and never wanted to be involved in a battle unless it was required to do so.

After a while, the Messenger of God gathered his friends in the Masjid and told them that they would be mobilized to conquer Mecca. He wanted them to be prepared for this end and warned his friends to conceal their preparations. The Muslims were all excited. It was especially remarkable to see the excitement of the people who had migrated from Mecca to Medina. They were going to conquer the lands they had been forced to leave.

In a short period of time, the Muslims completed their preparations. It was the first days of Ramadan. The Messenger of God left Medina for Mecca with ten thousand people, who were overexcited to return to Mecca. Soon after, the unbelievers of Mecca heard that they were rapidly nearing the city. The people of Mecca, who were not ready for any battle, became frightened as they did not believe that the Muslims would come so early. To learn the latest situation, they sent their leader Abu Sufyan and a few other people in the direction where the Muslims were headed. Abu Sufyan and his followers neared the place where the Muslims were staying at one night, and they were caught by the Muslims. They were rather bewildered. They did their best in order to escape. Upon learning the situation, Abbas went to the site, captured Abu Sufyan, and took him to the Messenger of God. Seeing what was happening, Umar immediately went to the tent of the Prophet and told him:

"O Messenger of God! Abu Sufyan applied terrible torture to both you and our friends. Let me kill him with my sword."

Abbas intervened to stop this, and the Messenger of God instructed Abbas so that the quarrel did not grow:

"Take Abu Sufyan to the guest tent. Bring him here in the morning."

The next morning, Abu Sufyan, accompanied by Umar, came to the tent of the Messenger of God. After Abu Sufyan entered into the tent, the Prophet asked him:

"O Abu Sufyan! Hasn't the time for you to say *La ilaha illallah, Muhammad'ur-Rasullulah* (There is no deity but God, Muhammad is the Messenger of God) come yet?

Abu Sufyan did not feel the power in himself to leave the idols. And he said:

"What will happen to my idols then? How can I give up Lat and Uzza?"

At this time, Umar was outside the tent listening to them. Becoming angry with these illogical words of Abu Sufyan, Umar said:

"O Abu Sufyan! You should thank God that you are in the tent of the Messenger of God. If you were outside, you could not utter such words."

Abu Sufyan was rather impressed by the gentle behavior of the Messenger of God even though he had caused big problems for him. Nevertheless, he could not manage to make that change. He demanded some time from him. In the meantime, Abbas intervened and said:

"O Abu Sufyan! What a pity for you! Be rational. Are you aware of what you are doing? Be Muslim before you are killed."

After a time of thinking Abu Sufyan made his decision and confessed his belief in God by reciting the *shahada*.[5] Later, he asked for per-

---

[5] There is no deity but God, Muhammad is the Messenger of God.

mission to leave and rapidly went to Mecca. He called those gathering around him in this way:

"O people of Quraysh! Here is the Messenger of God! They have come to us with a big army against which we cannot resist. I accepted Islam. Become Muslim and be saved. Anyone wishing to be safe can come to my house."

The people of Mecca, even the wife of Abu Sufyan, insulted him. Some rejected, yet the majority of the people of the Quraysh either went to his house or ran to the Ka'ba.

After this event, the Messenger of God and his Companions entered Mecca in magnificence. Prophet Muhammad, peace and blessings be upon him, stopped at the entrance of Mecca, addressed the people of Mecca, and commanded his commanders:

"Unless they attack you, you will not fight against them. You will not kill anyone."

The Messenger of God did not want anyone to be harmed except for a few people who performed extreme enmity towards the Muslim. Because he was the Messenger of God, he never cursed anyone who tortured Muslims.

He mounted his camel, Qaswa. He was both praying to God for all these blessings and reciting the *surah* al-Fath. The Messenger of God and his Companions together went to the Ka'ba. When it was time for noon prayer, Bilal went on top of the Ka'ba and called the *adhan*[6] with his magnificent voice. The eyes of all the Muslims, in particular those of the immigrants, filled with tears. In the Ka'ba, where they had been so close yet could not enter because of the torture of the unbelievers, the *adhan* was now being read. What a big blessing of God! After prayer, the Messenger of God gave a speech and declared a general amnesty at Mecca. Then he went to Hill of Safa. The people of Mecca came in big groups and declared their allegiances to him. They turned into a big crowd. The Messenger of God accepted the allegiances of the men while Umar was accepting those of the women. Later, Prophet Muhammad, peace and blessings be upon him, ordered the elimination from the Ka'ba all idols both inside and outside of it. The Messenger of God and his Companions, after staying a certain period of time at Ka'ba, returned to Medina.

---

[6] The call to prayer.

LET ME KILL HIM

After their victory, the wealth acquired as a result of the battle was distributed and everyone waited for their turn to come. It was the Messenger of God that was distributing the wealth. Everyone came to him one by one and took the share given by him. As he had been in all of his work, it was he who was the fairest of all. It was him, the Prophet of mercy who did not eat a piece of bread for days so that others could eat.

The division of wealth came to an end. God's Messenger was together with his friends, among whom was also Umar, at the place where the division of wealth was performed. They were about to leave when a man with hollow eyes appeared. Everyone thought that the man would ask the Messenger of God a question. The man came before him, stopped there, and addressed him in this way:

"That division of wealth should be fair, be fair!"

Everyone there was shaken. How could a Muslim address his Prophet in this way? Of course, one could not. How could such a thing be said to the one on whose honesty everybody, even the unbelievers agreed?

It was obvious that this person was a hypocrite because no Muslim would slander the Messenger of God. Knowing that this person was a hypocrite but not wanting to declare this among the people, the Messenger of God never changed his attitude and in a quite calm manner said:

"If it is not me who is the fair one, who could it be else? If I do not act fairly, I will be at a loss."

What the Messenger of God wanted to say with his words was this: If a Prophet is not fair, from whom can the people learn justice? In a place where there is no justice, people will be at a loss and disappointed.

The Companions were quite surprised. Umar could not wait and walked towards that man.

He wanted to tell him off. Turning to the Messenger of God, he said:

"O Messenger of God! Let me kill this man."

But he did not let him as he had never retaliated against someone for insulting him, but instead he prayed to God that they learn the truth. However, it was Umar who witnessed the event, and his heart could not bear such a slander against the fairest person ever. If he had let him, Umar would have killed that man right there. However, since the Prophet did not allow him to do so, he did not even touch him.

THE WORLD AND THE HEREAFTER

One day, Umar went to the room of God's Messenger in order to talk about certain issues. On one side of the room there was a processed leather, on the other side was a small bag holding a handful of barley, and on another corner of the room was a rush mat on which he slept. The rush mat that he slept on made a mark on his face. This scene deeply affected Umar. He went into tears. Before accepting Islam, Umar had never been seen crying. However, now he became so sensitive that whenever he was affected, he could not stop his tears from running. When the Messenger of God asked him why he was crying, Umar responded in this way:

"O Messenger of God! While kings are sleeping in their beds stuffed with down feathers, you sleep just on an old rush mat. And that rush mat made a mark on your blessed face. This made me cry."

Upon this, he looked at Umar and told him:

"O Umar! Wouldn't you want that the world is theirs and the Hereafter ours?

INCLUDE US IN YOUR PRAYERS

Craving for the Ka'ba, Umar wanted to go to Mecca for *umra*. He asked the Messenger of God for permission, and he allowed Umar to go. After giving permission he stood up and hugged Umar. Then he demanded from Umar something that would excite and please Umar for the rest of his life:

My friend, include us in your prayers.

The Messenger of God wanted Umar to pray for him. This word of the Prophet always excited and encouraged Umar. Whenever he recalled that day, Umar said: "Even if I had been granted the all world, I would not have been that happy."

THE PAIN OF SEPARATION

After the conquest of Mecca, God made it binding duty for the Muslims to make a pilgrimage. The Messenger of God wanted to implement this duty commanded by God. It had been ten years since the Migration. He told the Muslims to get ready for the hajj. He also wanted those Muslims living outside Medina to complete their preparations and gather at Medina. With the purpose of worshipping God, thousands of Muslims ran to Medina.

The Messenger of God along with thousands of Muslims whose hearts were filled with love for God and His Messenger left Medina for Mecca. They cried together in excitement *"labbayk*

Allahumma labbayk..."[7] Some also joined this holy journey half way to Mecca. On the fourth of Dhu'l-Hijja[8] on Sunday, the Messenger of God and the people of Medina reached Mecca. What a crowd it was! Accompanied by the people in Mecca and the people coming from the surrounding places, the number of those Muslims at Mecca exceeded one hundred thousand. Altogether they completed their hajj rituals. Those Muslims who had been with the Messenger of God since the beginning of calling people to Islam were much more excited and happy. The Ka'ba, where once they had to pray covertly because of the unbelievers, was now filled with the exclamations of *"Allahu Akbar"* coming from one hundred and twenty thousand people. Tears of joy were running from their eyes.

With the instruction of the Messenger of God, they gathered at Arafat. He provided advice to those who looked to him with great admiration and respect. This sermon was the last sermon of God's Messenger. With the last message, he

---

[7] My God! I came to You in compliance with Your invitation. You have no partner, not equivalent.

[8] The twelfth and final month in the Islamic calendar.

completed his mission of teaching all the principles of Islam to the all of humanity. This hajj became the first and the last hajj of the Prophet Muhammad, peace and blessings be upon him.

After completing their hajj, the Messenger of God and the Muslims of Medina returned to Medina. It was the eleventh year of the Migration and during the last days of May. The Prophet became ill, and his illness got increasingly worse. He had a high fever. He was not able to go to the Masjid to lead the congregational prayer. Instead, he assigned Abu Bakr, his loyal friend, to be the imam of the prayers. He made amends for all that had past with his Companions.

The day came. The blessed head of the Messenger of God was on the lap of Aisha, his wife. He found it very hard to breathe. He was at the same time praying, "My God! Accept me in Your holy friendship". He was living his very last moments in this world. From his blessed lips came the words *"ila'r-rafiq al-a'la"*[9] He looked at the ceiling and delivered his soul to the All-Merciful.

This painful news was heard by everyone in a very short time. The Muslims did not expect

---

[9]   To the Exalted Friend.

this painful news. Was it so easy to accept this? The person who provided them with the pleasure of Islam was not with them anymore. They were orphans now. To whom would they go to share their happiness and sadness?

Umar was among those who had been most deeply affected by the death of the Messenger of God. He was the son of Khattab, yet he got his real education, the education that made him Umar, from the Messenger of God. He reformed everything about himself—how to speak, how to act, and how to behave—in accordance with the warnings and suggestions of God's Messenger. The fact that he would not be able to see his Prophet made him mad. His intelligence that found solutions to any dire situation was no longer with Umar. He wanted wholeheartedly that this news was incorrect. Jumping up, he directly went to him. He looked at his blessed face and said:

"The Messenger of God has fainted and his faintness is quite heavy. But people cannot understand this."

Umar could neither utter that God's Messenger had died nor could not accept this news from anyone. He did not believe his own words either. All he wanted was to see him alive. Maybe he found some comfort in saying that he was still alive. It did not suffice him to say this to himself. Instead, because of his sadness and great concern, he raised his voice, yelling:

"Muhammad is not dead! I kill with my sword anyone who says Muhammad has died!"

Learning that the Messenger of God had passed to the eternal world, Abu Bakr came directly to his house and entered in his room. He lifted the cloth on his face. His lips trembling he said:

"O My friend!"

Tears running down his face, he kissed the forehead of the Messenger of God. That usual sweet smile was still on his face.

Abu Bakr said:

"May my mother and father be sacrificed for you, O Messenger of God! You are excellent in any situation, in life and in death."

While entering into the house of the Messenger of God, Abu Bakr heard Umar saying, "The Messenger of God has not died." Leaving the house, he directly went to the Masjid and called people who gathered there in this way:

"Whoever believes in Muhammad should know that Muhammad has died! Whoever worships God should know that God is the All-Living and Immortal One."

Later, he read the following verses of the *surah* Al Imran:

> Muhammad is but a Messenger, and Messengers passed away before him. If, then, he dies or is killed, will you turn back on your heels? Whoever turns back on his heels can in no way harm God. But God will (abundantly) reward the thankful ones (those who are steadfast in God's cause). (Al Imran, 3:144).

The speech and this verse of the Qur'an delivered by Abu Bakr enabled all of the Companions, especially Umar, to come to themselves. It was rather hard to acknowledge this painful fact. Yet, death was an inevitable reality as well. From that moment on, Umar never said again: "The Messenger of God has not died." He could not stop tears flowing, either.

THE FIRST CALIPH

T he Companions were used to consult with the Messenger of God on any problem, so after his union with his Creator, they did not know what to do. They had never thought about the inevitability of his death. They had never thought who would govern the state whose borders were expanding day by day after his death.

With the death of God's Messenger, they started to contemplate about who would be the new leader. Some proposed the idea that there could be two leaders, one of whom was from the Ansar and the other from the Muhajirun. Umar rejected this suggestion. He stood up and with his powerful oratory, he said:

"Two swords in just one scabbard are certain to touch each other."

Some of them did not understand his point: Therefore, he explained his thoughts in this way:

"In such case, the leaders may have a disagreement on the decisions they have to make. One leader may say something that totally disagrees with that of the other leader."

Most of the people gathered there found Umar right.

After a certain period of time debating these issues, they reached a compromise, and it was decided that Abu Bakr would be the first caliph. After this Abu Bakr came to the Masjid and sat on the *minbar* (pulpit). A few minutes before his speech, Umar stood up, thanked God, and then said:

"God granted the caliphate to the one who is the most appropriate and dutiful, to the loyal friend of the Messenger of God. You get up and declare your allegiance to him."

All Muslims stood up and declared their allegiance to the caliph one by one. Umar, who always best played the role of settling dissensions, once again displayed his role in preventing any discord among the Muslims on the issue of choosing the caliph.

The Caliph Abu Bakr appointed Umar, who contributed a lot to solving problems with his intelligence and bright ideas, as his helper. The son of Khattab, Umar was now both the confidant of Abu Bakr and his helper in solving the problems of the Muslims.

Umar showed great respect towards Abu Bakr since he was the closest loyal friend of the Prophet Muhammad, peace and blessings be upon him. One day, someone said something hinting that Umar was superior to Abu Bakr. Umar, who could not bear to hear such things, reacted harshly to this and said: "I swear by God that only one night of Abu Bakr is superior to the whole family of Umar."

WE NEED TO TAKE PRECAUTION

God, the Exalted One, sent His Messenger the verses of the Qur'an via Gabriel, one of the archangels. Gabriel read the verses of the Qur'an to the Messenger of God, and he had his scribes write them down. Many of the Companions learned these verses by heart. The vast majority of Companions preferred learning the verses by heart because they knew very well the utmost importance of this practice. It was also because in those times, written language was not well-developed, and they believed in the power of their memory. Thus, the number of those that memorized the Qur'an increased.

Anyone powerful enough used to join the battles in those times. Those memorized the Qur'an were also among the names that died in the battles. Umar realized this situation, and he began to worry that the probability that the number of people memorizing the Qur'an would decrease. He sought solutions to prevent this. He decided to discuss one of his solutions with Abu Bakr.

One day while they were talking about the problems of the Muslims, he explained his thoughts in this way:

"In the Battle of Yamamah, more than seventy people who memorized the whole Qur'an died. I fear that in the upcoming battles more people knowing Qur'an by heart will die. If this happens, the Qur'an will be incomplete. Therefore, we need to take some precautions right now. We shall collect the words of God and make them written.

Abu Bakr understood Umar's concern very well. However, he had a different concern as well. He said to Umar:

"How can I dare do something that the Messenger of God did not do?"

Since it was a big problem, Umar insisted on his opinion and said:

"My brother, I swear by God that this is a very propitious work."

Later he added the underlying reasons for his views in a detailed way. Thus, Umar persuaded Abu Bakr.

Upon this, Abu Bakr immediately called Zayd ibn Thabit to talk. Zayd was one of the scribes of God's Messenger. Abu Bakr explained to Zayd the concerns of Umar and his solution alike. Having listened to all of this, Zayd addressed Umar in this way:

"O Umar! How can we do something that the Messenger of God had never done before?"

Umar was about to answer this question, but Abu Bakr started to speak:

"I asked Umar the same question. Yet alone these words of his satisfied me. When the Messenger of God was alive, such a situation would not have occurred. If such a thing had happened, God would have sent the whole Qur'an again to the Messenger of God through revelation. Yet, now it is not possible for such a thing to come into being. That's why we need to take precaution."

Zayd had never thought about this before, and he found Umar's approach to be the right one. This important mission, upon the insistence of Umar, was given to Zayd by Abu Bakr. Zayd, after a series of long efforts to this end, achieved this mission. He meticulously collected the verses of the Qur'an that had been scattered so far. He collected all of them in the form of the Qur'an and handed it to the caliph. Thus, it was Zayd who was granted with the honor of collecting the verses of the Qur'an in written form.

Thanks to the sagacity of Umar, a gift given by God, one more important problem was settled as well. Umar contributed a lot to the solutions of such problems during the caliphate of Abu Bakr.

HEAVY BURDEN

I t had been thirteen years since the Migration. Abu Bakr had been the caliph of the
Muslims for two years. Despite his age, he
worked all day and night for the Muslims, and
so he was rather exhausted. For the last days, he
could not serve as the imam in the congregation. He assigned Umar as the deputy imam.

Abu Bakr felt too exhausted because of his
deteriorating health. Foreseeing that he would
die, Abu Bakr did not want the same problems
arise when the time came to choose the leader of
the state. He wanted to prevent the dissidence
that would divide the Muslims after his death.
To this end, he wanted to solve this problem at
once. Therefore, with the approval of the prominent names among the Companions, he wanted

to assign one of his Companions the role of caliph after him. The first name that came to his mind was, of course, Umar, who was his biggest helper and who contributed a lot to the solutions of many problems with his bright ideas and diligence. It was also because Abu Bakr had known Umar a long time ago. He was aware of the big transformation Umar experienced with his acceptance of Islam. So it was Umar whom Abu Bakr wholeheartedly wanted to see as the caliph. Before explaining this wish to people, Abu Bakr wanted to share the idea with his close friends. He first asked one of the prominent names of Companions, Abdurrahman ibn Awf:

"What do you think about Umar's being caliph?"

"You ask me about the person whom you know better than me!"

Such was Abdurrahman's answer. He was right because before the death of the Messenger of God, Abu Bakr and Umar were always with him, and they knew each other very well.

Upon this, Abu Bakr said:

"Yes, I may know him better than you, but I also want to learn your opinion about it."

Then Abdurrahman ibn Awf added:

"I swear that he is the most appropriate to be caliph among the Companions."

Abu Bakr was pleased with this response. He thought that he was right in his decision to designate Umar as the caliph. After this talk, Abu Bakr told Abdurrahman ibn Awf not to talk about this to anyone until they came to a decision.

Afterwards, Abu Bakr called his close friend Uthman ibn Affan. He directed the same questions to him as well. Uthman ibn Affan said these:

"It is you who knows him best!"

Upon this, Abu Bakr insisted on learning his opinion concerning the issue and said:

"O Abu Abdullah! You are right, but I still want to learn your opinion about this."

"Everyone knows that he is the genuine and the unique one."

Satisfied with this answer, Abu Bakr replied:

"O Uthman, may God have mercy on you! If it had not been Umar, I would have certainly designated you as the caliph. After this talk, Abu Bakr warned him as well not to tell anyone.

Abu Bakr went on asking the ideas of the pioneering names among the Ansar and the Muhajirun about the selection of Umar as the next caliph. They also approved the caliphate of Umar. Hearing all of these opinions, Abu Bakr's concerns were allayed. He thanked his Creator for granting him with the opportunity to choose the right name. Some people, hearing that Umar would be chosen as the caliph, said that he was strict nature. Abu Bakr then persuaded them with these words:

"Umar is one of the most propitious and best among the people of God."

He knew that although Umar was rather tough against injustice and violence, but he was rather gentle when it came to any matter related to religion and kindness.

After these discussions, Abu Bakr called Uthman and told him to write his will that would be dictated by Abu Bakr. Within this will, he declared that it was time for his death and that after him he wanted the Muslims to show allegiance to Umar. Later, he wanted Uthman to read this will to the people. Among the listeners nobody rejected his will. Having watched this scene, Abu Bakr came and asked the Muslims there:

"O Muslims! I suggest you accept as the caliph the person who is not my relative. Now, I suggest Umar ibn Khattab as the caliph. Do you accept this person with complete peace and comfort?"

People there altogether said:

"Yes, we accept."

"Listen and obey him. I swear God that I did my best to choose the most appropriate person," he said, and upon this statement, the people present replied:

"We will listen and obey him."

Later Abu Bakr called Umar and told him:

"I have chosen you as the caliph from among the Companions of the Messenger of God."

He then gave him some advice. Abu Bakr felt that the big burden on his shoulder was no longer there. It was because he designated as caliph the person whom he most trusted and for whom he could be the guarantor of any actions.

After this event, Abu Bakr became sicker and sicker, and he was no longer able to get out of his bed. It was time for him to reach his

Beloved Friend. He delivered his noble soul to God and left this world.

Now, it was Umar who was the new caliph of the Muslims. That big burden was on his shoulders. Although he did not want to be the caliph, he took on this responsibility only with the intention of not avoiding the mission given to him. He shared these thoughts with the people gathered in the Masjid after burying Abu Bakr:

"O people! I am just an ordinary man. Even though I did not want it, I accepted this mission so that I did not break the heart of the caliph of the Messenger of God. You can be sure about the fact that I will do my best for the good of you. I swear to the Creator of the Ka'ba that I will govern the Muslims in the fairest and the most appropriate way."

DECISIONS ARE THE RESULT OF CONSULTATION

D uring the days of the Messenger of God, Islam had rapidly spread in the Arabian Peninsula and in particular, after the conquest of Mecca people accepted Islam in large groups and numbers.

The same thing happened during the caliphate of Abu Bakr. Yet, these were accompanied by arduous efforts to prevent the spread of Islam as well. In this period, Islamic armies had to combat the two biggest super powers of the world. Abu Bakr initiated military raids to the lands that were under the domination of the Byzantines. He also started military actions against the despotic Sassanid Persian Empire.

Umar proceeded with the conquests after Abu Bakr. In Persia, activities preventing Islam increased more and more. Therefore, the Islamic army was prepared with the purpose of responding to and halting these anti-Islamic activities. A commander needed to be assigned at the head of this army. Umar had the authority to directly appoint the commander himself, yet he wanted to choose the commander through consultation just like the Messenger of God and Abu Bakr had always done. He wholeheartedly believed in the rewards of consultation. Therefore, he gathered with the prominent Companions to exchange ideas.

All of the important names among the Companions participated in the meeting. Some demanded that Umar himself be the commander of the army while some others said:

"It would be more appropriate for Umar to stay at the leadership of the state."

Everybody agreed upon this view. So they decided on another Companion to be sent as the commander. But who was it?

During the meeting, Sa'd ibn Abi Waqqas's letter, which he sent from the Hawazin to state his views related to the situation, reached the Muslims. Umar had sent Sa'd ibn Abi Waqqas to the Hawazin region to collect alms.

Hearing the name of Sa'd, the Companions in total agreement told Umar:

"Here, you have just found the appropriate person!"

Later they asked themselves that why they did not think about Sa'd before.

Upon this, Umar called Sa'd to Medina. He appointed him as the chief commander of the Islamic army. Later he told him this:

"O Sa'd! Never feel proud of yourself that you are the uncle of the Messenger of God. God rids all badness only through goodness. Whether one person is superior or not is determined when that person reaches his Creator. Do not fear the abundance of the enemy, but fear God."

Umar later gave advice to Sa'd on how to build a plentiful and successful army:

"You all must regularly perform your prayers! There should not be any soldier in your army that commits a sin! Remove those committing sin from your army! Just act in the same way the Messenger of God did! Never stop being patient!"

After the advice of Umar, Sa'd ibn Abi Waqqas left Medina with the soldiers under his command. They united with the soldiers that were in Persian lands, and then they altogether built their headquarters. The struggle was going to be against the Sassanid Empire, one of the most powerful empires of the time. They had a very powerful army consisting of a hundred thousand people as well. The commander of the army was Rostam Farrokhzad, who was famous for his heroism.

This combat was of critical importance in the sense that the message of Islam would reach many people in this way as until now the Sassanid Empire had obstructed the spread of Islam. Just as in the other battles, the Muslims did not prefer fighting. For this reason, they sent envoys to talk to the Sassanid leaders, but it was no use. The Sassanids were highly confident about their army. The next day, the battle began and the Muslim army won with the help of God. This battle was written in history as the Battle of al-Qadisiyyah.

WHO IS NEXT?

It was the sixteenth year of the Migration. After the conquest of Syria, military units in this region were directed towards the west of the region. The Muslim soldiers under the command of Abu Ubayda ibn Jarrah surrounded Jerusalem. Militarily speaking, they dominated. The officials of Jerusalem understood that they would not be able to fight against the Islamic army and handed the city to the Muslims. Now, Jerusalem was also conquered. However, the priests did not want to deliver the keys of the city to the Muslim commanders. They wanted the caliph to come himself and after the guarantee had been given by the caliph, they said they would hand over the keys. The conqueror of Jerusalem, Abu Ubayda, informed Umar about the situation by letter. The Caliph Umar talked about the issue with the majority of the Companions. Some of the Companions believing that there was no need for Umar to go there, said:

"It is not appropriate for the great caliph to go there just to take the keys! It would be much better for the commanders there to take the keys."

However, the vast majority of the prominent names among the Companions said:

"If our caliph accepts their call to Jerusalem, it will help us in winning the hearts of people of Jerusalem."

Thus, Umar decided to go to Jerusalem. Yet, there was an important problem. That great caliph had spent everything he owned in the name of God, and he had no mount to carry him there. He borrowed a camel from the *Bayt al-mal*[10]. They intended to first stop by the conquered Damascus; then they would go to Jerusalem. Umar had his slave with him as well. In the early morning, they set off with only one camel. After a while, Umar stopped his camel

---

[10]   The financial institution responsible for the administration of taxes.

and got off. His slave, thinking that Umar was in need of something, approached him. Right at that moment, Umar told his slave:

"Come, it is your turn.

His slave had no idea what he was talking about. What was the turn that had come to him? He looked at the caliph implying that he did not understand anything. Being more explicit, Umar said:

"Come and get on this camel; it is my turn to walk now."

His slave thought he had misunderstood Umar. Umar reiterated his words:

"Come and get on the camel!"

"How could that be, master?" said his slave, and he did not want to get on the camel.

His slave did not complain about walking, but Umar, who became more sensitive after accepting Islam, could not let that continue. He could not ride on the camel while his slave was walking all the time. Umar was quite adamant about this.

His slave refused to get on the camel. But it was no use. It was Umar, and his slave also knew very well that Umar would not let go of something once he really decided on it. There-fore, he did not put up very much resistance. The great caliph helped his slave mount the camel.

They went on their journey; he was on foot, his slave on camel. Later, seeing that Umar was very tired of walking, the slave wanted Umar to get on the camel. So, Umar rode the camel. Yet after a certain period of time, he again wanted his slave to take the camel, and thus it was again the slave's turn. After a while they changed again. In this way, they went on their journey and approached Damascus. It was the slave's turn to get on the camel. However, Umar's slave did not want to ride the camel now because he did not want people see him on the camel while the great caliph was on foot. He knew that people would find this bizarre. But, again it was Umar. He would not stop doing something right just because of the possibility that people would find it weird. This time a bit louder he shouted:

"I order you. Get on this camel right now!"

There was nothing the slave could do now. Unwillingly, he mounted the camel. The slave was on the camel while Umar was holding its halter. There was a stream in front of them that they had to cross. The slave on the camel attempted to request that Umar ride the camel across the stream, but Umar did not accept this offer. With one hand the caliph held the halter of the camel while he rolled up his trouser legs with the other. Then they crossed the stream. In the same way, the slave on the camel and the caliph on foot, they entered into the city. Those who did not know Umar assumed that the one on the camel was the caliph while the one who kept the halter of the camel was the slave. Abu Ubayda and some other Muslims, who knew that the caliph would come, had come to the city of Jabiyah to meet him.

Some among those that came there to meet the caliph said:

"If you had ridden a horse instead of a camel and dressed new clothes instead of the worn-out ones, you would have much influence over the people of this country."

These words made Umar very angry. He said to those coming there:

"God honored us with Islam. If we look for honor and glory in something else other than the things God granted us, God makes us despicable.

To him, the real honor and glory was being a Muslim. These words became more meaningful when they were uttered by Umar, who both experienced the ugliness of the pre-Islamic paganism and came to be one of the closest friends of the Messenger of God after accepting Islam.

With the agreement made there, Jerusalem was delivered to the Muslims. The keys of the city were handed in Umar. The people of Jerusalem were in peace now. They had heard that Umar would do his best to watch over those under his protection and to be fair to everyone. After the agreement, he addressed the people of Jerusalem in this way:

"You can maintain your lives as you wish. From now on, you are under our protection. You can be sure that we will protect your lives and possessions as if they were ours."

These words gave the people of Jerusalem much relief. After signing the agreement, Umar went to Jerusalem and entered into the Church of Al-Qiyamah there. He was met by the patriarch, the leader of the Christians. He asked him:

"Is there a place where I can perform prayer?"

The patriarch replied:

"You can perform it anywhere in the church."

The caliph said:

"No, I don't want to perform prayer within the church."

And he performed his prayer in a place that was close to the exit of the church.

The patriarch could not understand why Umar hadn't wanted to perform his prayer within the church. He thought to himself: "Maybe he thought that the church was not cleaned well."

Turning to Umar, he asked:

"Sir, our church has just been cleaned. Any place of it is quite clean. Why did you prefer the place that is near to the exit door?"

Upon this, Umar said:

"If I had performed prayers in the church, the other Muslims would have done so, and they would have turned it into a mosque. However, I want this place to be the place where you can easily perform your own prayers."

The patriarch was heavily influenced by these words of Umar. He thought, "These Muslim people show a great respect toward our religion." Without losing any time, he went to kiss the hands of Umar who behaved in such a decent way.

It was not enough for Umar, and he demanded the text of the agreement. Later, he added to the text the clause that read: "The Muslims shall not gather in the church for prayers and shall not read *adhan* in the church." The Christians were influenced by the fact that the caliph of the Muslims even changed the clauses of the agreement text in order to protect the rights of the people who were not of their own religion. Some of them recited the *shahada* there and became Muslims. Being affected by this attitude of the caliph, the officials asked:

"Do you have any demand?"

Umar wanted the patriarch to show him a place for them to build a mosque. The patriarch showed the holy hill where God addressed Jacob. Umar went up the hill and started to clear this place with his hands. Seeing him, the people also began to work. In a short time, they organized the place and made it ready for a mosque to be built. Umar ordered a mosque to be built in that spot, and for a certain time he controlled the progress there. Later, he turned back to Medina.

HOW CAN I DIFFER FROM MY TWO FRIENDS?

C onquests continued rapidly. During his period of the caliphate, many countries were
conquered. The Islamic lands reached more
than two million square kilometers, and the trea-
suries were all filled. None of this ever changed
Umar. He was still the modest one who never felt
proud of himself. With the excellent institutions
he built, Umar managed well the Islamic state.

Despite his age, he still exerted great efforts
to solve the problems of the Muslims. He even
forgot to sleep and eat when he was deeply involved in solving the problems of the Muslims.
This worried his daughter Hafsa, and she feared
that her father would be ill. The Caliph Umar
also dressed in quite a humble way. Although he

was the caliph of the expansive Islamic world, he wore clothes with twelve coverings. His daughter Hafsa wished her father would dress better and eat better food so that he could do his work much better. However, she could not tell him this.

One day, messengers from the neighboring countries came. Umar met them wearing his usual twelve piece clothing. The talks lasted a long time, so he was not able to eat anything for many hours. It was very late when he arrived home. Hafsa, seeing her father exhausted, could not stand it and said:

"My dear father, messengers from other countries are always coming. You meet with new committees and talk with them. Wouldn't it be better if you renewed your clothes and ate better food since God has given us plenty of food?"

Hearing these from his daughter, Umar was very surprised. He asked her:

"Don't you remember those difficulties the Messenger of God and Abu Bakr had faced?"

He reiterated this question many times.

Seeing that she broke the heart of her father, Hafsa became very sad. Crying, she hugged her father. Later, turning to his daughter Umar said:

"I swear you will not say something like this again!"

Referring to the Messenger of God and Abu Bakr, he said:

"How can I differ from my two friends? If I want to be with them in the Hereafter, I have to live like them in this world, too."

IT WAS ONLY YESTERDAY

The Caliph Umar gathered people in the Masjid with the purpose of informing them. As in the time of the Messenger of God, the mosques acted as places where the problems of the Muslims were settled. The one who managed the state addressed the people from the *minbar* concerning the important events and news.

The Masjid was full as usual. People had left their works and come to listen to the sermon of the caliph. The Caliph Umar went to the *minbar* without hesitation. He was a very punctual person. He never liked people wasting their time. He informed them about important events and explained to them how to act. Later, he stopped and said something that was not related to the topic.

"You were just a herdsman who was herding his father's animals."

The people present were a bit surprised by these words. Nobody was able to understand why Umar uttered such words and how this statement related to the topic of the sermon. He finished his sermon and left the *minbar*. Then, people started to leave the Masjid. However, in their minds there were these words of Umar: "You were just a herdsman who was herding his father's animals." Nobody other than Umar could answer this question in their minds. They went to Umar and asked:

"O Chief of Believers, what did you mean by these words?"

That great caliph who governed the large geographical expanse gave such an answer:

"During my speech, it came to my mind that I was the caliph. I did not feel proud of this. However, I feared that I felt pride unconsciously. Therefore, in order to give advice to myself and to remember my past, I said such a thing."

IS THERE A BETTER
SLAVE THAN ME?

One day, Ahnaf ibn Qays went to visit Umar with the leading names of the Arabs. At the moment they arrived, Umar was gathering up the pieces of his clothing and running. Seeing that Ahnaf was coming towards him, Umar said:

"Come, come, you run too. It ran towards that side."

Ahnaf could not understand what he meant, thus he asked in wonder:

"Who ran away?"

"A camel that belongs to the state. You know how many people have a right on that camel."

One of those that came with Ahnaf said:

"You are the caliph. You can call the slaves to catch the camel."

This made Umar mad because he did not have such an approach in his understanding of life. He did not see the caliphate as the position he could reach but as the means of serving the Muslims. Thus he never thought, "I am the caliph, dealing with such things is not my job." He was ready to make any sacrifice in order to protect the smallest rights of the Muslims. Turning towards the person that uttered these words, Umar said:

"Is there a better slave than me?"

With this, he meant that he would work like a slave in order to protect the rights of his people.

THE CALIPH THAT CARRIES A SACK

U mar sometimes changed his clothes in order not to be recognized by the people, and sometimes in his daily clothing, he wandered around Medina. He even acted as the watchman at night in order to be sure that people lived under good conditions and in peace. Moreover, he personally helped those in need.

On one of those nights when he had worked a lot and was exhausted, he returned home with his helper, Aslam. On the way, Aslam said:

"Tonight it is too cold, isn't it my master?"

Umar replied:

"Yes, it is really cold."

Then he saw a fire in the far distance and asked Aslam:

"Aslam, did you see the fire there, too?"

"Yes, master I saw it too."

"Who could have lit a fire?"

Aslam did not know.

Umar went on saying:

"They must be people who feel cold at this time of the night. They could be on a journey. Maybe they could not go on their journey because it is night and made a fire as a result of that cold. They may need help."

"Yes, they may."

Umar said: "Let's go there then."

Thus, they started to walk towards the fire. The people were quite far away from them, but they could have been in need of help. They both talked and walked towards the place where the fire was lit. It was in the middle of night, and there was nobody else on the streets. People had already gone into their homes and were even sleeping. However, Umar and Aslam were walking in the cold at that late hour of the night. Despite the cold, they felt happy in the very inner of themselves. It was because they would be able to help people who were in need of help.

The scene they encountered was not like anything they could have ever imagined. Around the fire sat an old woman and crying children. On the fire was a saucepan with boiling water in it. The children were waiting around the saucepan and often opened the lid of the saucepan and looked in it.

The woman and the children didn't know who these people were. They both feared and were surprised to see them there. Umar addressed the woman:

"Do you mind us coming?"

The woman said:

"If you can solve our problem, you can come."

The woman did not understand that it was the caliph of the Muslims because she had never seen him before. Besides, the behavior of Umar, who dressed like the others, was not different than an ordinary person.

Umar asked in wonder:

"What are you doing here?"

The old woman answered:

"Since we have no home, we had to be outside under this cold. I am trying to warm the children with this fire."

"Why are the children crying?"

"Because of hunger. I could not feed them."

"What is it boiling in the saucepan? Isn't it food?"

The woman opened the lid of the saucepan and showed them what was in it. Then she started to tell them what she was doing:

"We have no food to eat, so I put a stone in it instead. I am all the time mixing the water with a spoon. In this way, I am trying to keep the children busy. If I can manage this for a bit longer, they may go to sleep. Since they are starving, I cannot stop their crying in any other way."

The woman continued:

"God will certainly call the Caliph Umar to account because of this."

Umar was surprised and said:

"How could Umar know about your situation?"

The old woman, in rather a sad manner, responded to Umar:

"Why did he want to govern us if he did not know about our situation and want to help us?"

Hearing this, Umar was startled. He looked at this helper, Aslam. They immediately left. The woman was surprised by this. Two foreigners came to her in the middle of the night, listened to her, and then left them without saying anything.

Leaving the woman, Umar and Aslam walked towards the storehouse of the city. Umar was under the influence of the words of the woman. He was walking so fast that Aslam found it very hard to keep up with him. At last, they arrived at the storehouse. They put in a sack all that the woman and children could need.

Aslam now understood what Umar was doing. He wanted to carry the sack, but Umar stopped him saying:

"No Aslam, I must carry this myself."

"How could that be my master, I am your helper. I can't let you carry this sack."

However, Umar, in a decisive manner said:

"Put that sack on my back, now."

When Aslam said:

"O my master, how could I do this? Please let me carry it."

Umar responded:

"I am responsible for these people. It is I who need to find the solution to their problems. He lifted the sack and put it on his back."

The Caliph Umar, in the middle of that freezing cold night, put the sack on his back, went on walking, and in the end they arrived at the campsite. It was the same as they had left it. The children had not gone to sleep yet because of their hunger, and the expression on the woman's face became more sensitive now. She was continuing to mix the water in the saucepan, and said again:

"God will hold Umar responsible for this."

The woman and the children were even more surprised to see Umar and Aslam return. Their surprise could be seen in their eyes. Who were these strangers who came to them a second time at that late hour of the night?

Umar, with the help of Aslam, put the sack which was full of food on the ground. The fire under the saucepan was now dying out. Asking the permission of the old woman, Umar blew on the fire. Aslam put the timbers he collected on the fire. Umar went on blowing on the fire until the timbers began to burn. Later, he opened the sack. He took some of the food, put it in the saucepan, and added some water. He was both mixing the meal and blowing on the fire so that the meal was cooked fast and well. Very soon the meal was ready.

Umar, again with the help of Aslam, took the meal from the fire. He knew that the children would not wait for the meal to get cold. He immediately put some food in the dishes. The children were shy so he held the children's hands and told them to eat the meal. He children were very hungry. The more they ate, the more Umar added in their dishes.

A time later, the children were full and started to play amongst themselves. The woman was happy seeing the children playing in a great joy. She thought to herself: "How could I have fed the children if these people had not helped us? I cannot repay them however much I thank them."

The woman, looking at Umar of whose identity she was not aware, said:

"You should have been our caliph instead of Umar."

Umar asked:

"Why do you say so?"

The old woman replied:

"Because he is unaware of the situation of his people and does not help people who are in need. Nevertheless, you helped us even though you didn't know us."

So Umar said:

"Tomorrow, you go to the Caliph Umar and tell him about your situation. Maybe he will put you on a stipend so that the children can eat well, play, and enjoy life like their peers."

In the meantime, the children, feeling full, fell asleep near the fire. The woman thanked and prayed for them. Umar and Aslam, happy with the situation of the woman and children, went home.

The next morning, the woman decided to go to the Caliph Umar. On the road, she wondered whether the caliph would accept her wishes or not. Deep in these thoughts and concerns, she asked the people there the caliph's room. Later, she knocked on the door and came in only to see what? The caliph was no one else but the man who carried the sack on his back in the middle of the night and cooked for them.

STIPEND TO ALL CHILDREN

One night, Umar was again on the streets in the middle of a night with his friend Abdurrahman ibn Awf with the purpose of seeing the living conditions of people and finding solutions to their problems. The city was deeply quiet. Almost all the people were asleep. In this deep stillness, they heard a child crying. They turned towards the direction of that voice. The Caliph Umar said to his friend Abdurrahman:

"You wait for me here. I shall go to the place where the crying is coming from."

"Okay," said Abdurrahman.

Umar walked in the direction of the voice. The closer he got, the better he could hear the voice. So it was not difficult to find the house that the crying came from. He approached the house and knocked on the door. A young woman opened the door. Umar asked:

"Is it your child that is crying?"

"Yes."

"Fear God and take care of your child," he said and left that house.

Then the cry of the child disappeared. Umar, with rapid steps, came to his friend Abdurrahman. They were discussing the ways to solve people's problems. Umar talked about the projects he would implement for the people who were under his administration. Soon after, they heard that cry again. The caliph's anger increased. He stopped speaking. He again headed towards the house from where that voice was coming. This time he knocked hard at the door. The door was again opened by the mother of the crying child. Umar, in anger, warned the mother:

"Why aren't you taking care of your child? Take well care of the child and do not let the child cry."

The woman didn't know Umar, so she looked at him in surprise. Seeing that he was very angry, she didn't say anything. Umar closed the door and left that house. He came to his friend

Abdurrahman who was waiting for him. They waited for a while there and then left. They performed an ablution. For a certain period of time, they performed their prayers. They prayed to God for both themselves and the other Muslims.

It was almost midnight. The streets were now calmer. Umar and Abdurrahman were about to leave when they heard that child crying again. Umar told Abdurrahman:

"Why is she making that little child cry? I will go there again and talk to the mother of that child."

So he started to walk rapidly towards that house. He was even angrier now. He knocked at the door in quite a harsh manner. The woman opened the door and was startled. The same person came for the third time to tell her to stop her child from crying. She wondered who that man was. Not knowing Umar, the woman murmured to herself: "He must have been disturbed by the voice of the child and couldn't sleep."

Umar said angrily:

"Why is that child still crying?"

"I can't stop him. He stops crying for a while then starts again."

"Why doesn't he stop crying? Is he sick?"

"No he is not!"

While Umar and the mother were talking in front of the door, the child was still crying inside.

Umar, pointing at the child crying inside, asked:

"But why is he still crying then?"

"He is crying because he wants to nurse, but I want to wean him."

"But is he older than two?"

"No, he isn't."

"Then, why are you trying to wean him?"

"I have heard that the Caliph Umar puts all children that are weaned on a stipend. So I want to wean my child so that he can be on the stipend."

Hearing this, Umar couldn't believe his ears. He was totally shocked. He asked himself: "How many more children have been weaned because of me?"

Umar put the children who stopped nursing or passed the age of nursing on a stipend thinking that their expenses of food and other needs would be too much for their families. However, people started to wean their children even when they needed nursing so that they could be on a stipend. The caliph had not made a mistake with this decision because he had good intentions in doing it and could not have guessed that it would bring about such results.

The woman was trying to understand the murmuring of Umar. Turning towards him, she asked:

"Did you say something to me?"

Umar was still in shock. Without giving any answer, he left and turned back to his friend. Abdurrahman was so surprised because Umar's face had turned pure white, and he was constantly murmuring something. Getting closer to his friend, Abdurrahman heard Umar saying to himself: "O Umar how many children have been weaned because of you!"

He asked:

"What are you saying O Umar?"

"Abdurrahman, tomorrow we are going to immediately reverse the decision we have made."

"Which decision?"

"The decision to put the children who stopped nursing on salary stipend."

"How will we change it?"

"We will put all children on salary stipend regardless of their age or whether they are being nursed or not. Thus, we will be able to prevent some mothers from letting their children go hungry."

When Umar decided on something, he would certainly implement it without losing any time. In the early morning, the first thing he did was to change that policy and from that day on, he ordered that every newborn child be put on salary stipend. Furthermore, the first population census was performed during his time.

THE CALIPH, WATCHMAN OF THE CARAVAN

T he caliph, paying an utmost attention to the control of the streets, saw a caravan one night. Without losing time, he directly went to that caravan, but he could not see that anyone was awake. Everyone in the caravan was sleeping. He again went around the caravan but couldn't find anyone to talk to. He wanted to learn who they were, from where they were coming, and whether they needed anything.

He realized from the things in the caravan that they were Christians. He was the caliph of the Muslims, but he worked day and night not only for the happiness of the Muslims but for anyone that was living within his dominion. He considered himself responsible for maintaining the happiness of these people. He adopted the principle that "If a camel is lost at the edge of the Euphrates, I fear that God will hold me responsible for this." He very often reiterated this statement. Umar felt accountable for the loss of any animal within the boundaries of his domination, and would do anything for anyone even if they were not Muslims. He knew it also very well that his own people, the Muslims, would not harm them in any way. Yet, the caravan has stopped at a very busy place full of people coming and going. So, it was possible that the valuable properties of the caravan would be stolen since it had no watchman under this darkness.

Therefore he made a decision and went directly to the house of Abdurrahman. He knocked at his door in a hurry. Waking up Abdurrahman, immediately got out of his bed and opened the door. The caliph first said:

"*Salamun alaykum* (peace be upon you) O Abdurrahman!"

Abdurrahman responded to Umar:

"*Alaykum salam* (upon you be peace). Come in. I hope everything is fine."

"No, I won't come in. Get ready at once; we need to go somewhere together."

"Where are we going?"

"A caravan has stopped on the outskirts of the city. They stopped there and all went to sleep. There is no watchman to protect them."

"From where are they coming and where are they going?"

"I don't know Abdurrahman. They all went to sleep. I understood from their belongings that they are Christians. I am afraid of their being harmed. Get ready! We shall go and protect them."

"Okay, I am coming right now."

They left the house and walked rapidly. They came to the caravan at last. Thinking that people in the caravan were tired, they did not wake up anyone. They stood in front of the caravan and waited. They both had no sleep at all.

Before they arrived, the watchmen of the caravan had already fallen asleep. After a while, one of the watchmen woke up and looked around. He realized that the other young people who were chosen as the watchmen went to sleep just as he did. Half awake, half sleepy, he thought: "Everyone is sleeping so I shall also sleep." Right at that moment, he saw Umar and Abdurrahman. He did not know whether they were real or not. He was so tired and sleepless that he couldn't even find the power to get up. Even though he didn't want to go to sleep, his eyelids just closed.

However, after a while, he woke up very worried. He thought that the two people in front of him could be thieves who came to steal the property of the caravan. He stared at them.

Later, he realized that those people were not thieves and that they were just sitting there. He thought, "If they had any ill-intention, they would have robbed our caravan. The head of the caravan must have paid them to watch over us." He wanted to wake up the head of the leader and to learn about these guys. But then he gave up. "There is no need to warn the head of the caravan. Everybody will wake up soon anyway. I ask him when they are all awake. I shall sleep a bit more before it is morning. Tomorrow we have a long journey; I need rest," he thought.

During that time, Umar and Abdurrahman were both talking and watching the caravan. The darkness of the night had now disappeared, and the sky had begun to turn blue. Those in the caravan started to wake up. It was about to be morning, and Umar and his friend saw people in the caravan waking up, and so they started to get ready for the morning prayer. Umar told Abdurrahman:

"It is about to be morning, and people in the caravan are also getting up. So there is no more need for us. Let's go to the city for prayer."

They cleaned their clothing of the dirt and went towards the city. At that time, the young man saw that the leader of the caravan was now awake, went to him, and explained to him the things he had seen that night. And he asked the head of the caravan:

"Did you hire the two guys who were waiting for our caravan?"

The head of the caravan had no idea what that man was talking about and asked:

"About whom are you speaking?"

"I am talking about the two strangers who watched the caravan the whole night."

The head of the caravan was surprised.

"No, I did not assign anyone other than you to watch the caravan."

The young man thought that he was mistaken. If those people were not there for the protection of the caravan, then they must have been thieves. He was overwhelmed by his sleep and couldn't catch those thieves. Worried, he told the head of the caravan:

"Then they must have been thieves, and when all the people were sleeping, they must have stolen our valuable things."

The head of the caravan was also surprised to hear this. He told everyone to look over their possession and tell him if there was something missing. All people in the caravan checked their belongings and found that nothing was stolen.

These two mysterious people were not thieves then. The head of the caravan told the people around him:

"If they are not thieves, they have come to protect us."

Then, turning to the young man, he asked:

"Could you recognize them if you saw them again?

"Yes, I could. I was sleepy when I saw them, but I remember their faces."

The head of the caravan said:

"They can't have gone very far. Be quick and find these men. Learn about who they are and why they came to watch our caravan."

The young man agreed and went all around the caravan trying to see in which direction those two men had gone. While looking around, he saw two men walking towards the city. They must have been the two men he was looking for. He immediately ran after them and secretly followed them.

Everyone was now awake in the caravan. The head of the caravan told everyone what the young man told him. All the people were in wonder now.

Everyone was asking each other:

"Who were these men and why had they protected them?"

Yet, none of them could find its answer at all.

The young man who was following Umar and Abdurrahman on the road asked the Muslims they encountered who these two people were.

The first man said:

"Don't you know him? He is the Caliph Umar. And the other is one of his closest friends, Abdurrahman ibn Awf."

The young man couldn't believe his ears. He thought, "That man must be making fun of me." How could that great head of state leave his warm bed and come in the middle of the night to watch a caravan of people whom he had never seen before?

He continued to ask others about their identity. All of them gave him the same answer.

"They are the Caliph Umar and his friend Abdurrahman."

Finally, believing what he had been told, the young man ran to the caravan and directly went to their leader. The people in the caravan were still talking about this. Seeing the young man coming, the head of the caravan asked in excitement:

"Have you been able to learn the identity of those people waiting for us at night?"

"Yes, I did. But you will not believe me if I tell you who they are."

The curiosity of the people increased when they heard this.

"Those who were watching the caravan were the leader of the Muslims, Umar and his friend."

After this, everybody fell silent. It was the old head of the caravan who was the most surprised. Since he travelled most among them, he heard the name of Umar everywhere he went.

"The head of state, Umar, who made the world trembled with his power and conquered new countries, acted as the watchman for the caravan of those who were not even of his own religion. That was unbelievable," he thought.

Everyone in the caravan found it very hard to believe that great caliph had come to protect them. After the first shock, the head of the caravan gathered everyone and told them:

"O my friends; that exemplary behavior of Umar derives from his religion, Islam. Therefore, I will find Umar and accept Islam."

Then, he directly went to the streets of Medina to find Umar. Seeing that the head of caravan went to find the caliph, those in the caravan followed him, saying:

"We want to be Muslims, too."

Altogether they asked where Umar was and finally found him. They talked with him. Then they recited the *shahada* and accepted Islam.

JUSTICE IS THE MAIN PILLAR OF PROPERTY

One day, a disagreement arose between Ubay ibn Ka'b and Umar. Ubay said to Umar: "O Caliph of the Messenger of God, you are doing me an injustice."

Umar, however, was saying that he was right. The best way to find a solution was to go to the *qadi* (judge) of Medina. At that time it was Zayd ibn Thabit who acted as the *qadi* of Medina. The caliph and Ubay went before Zayd. When they arrived, Zayd stood up out of respect for Umar and asked the caliph to take his seat. That did not mean that he would favor Umar in his decision-making. However, this act made Umar angry. All of a sudden, Umar told Zayd:

"No, Zayd, no! You have done an injustice just at the very beginning. I did not come here as the caliph but as the one to be judged. Since it is not certain for now who is right and who is wrong, we should be considered at the same position."

Therefore, Zayd sat down on his place. They also took their seats in front of Zayd, and so the trial went on.

Umar was the perfect symbol of justice. He said, "Justice is the main pillar of property," and in each phase of his life, he always put this principle into practice. Furthermore, he did not take any offence at being judged before a judge whom was assigned to this post himself. Today, thanks to his attitude, despite the fact that more than 14 centuries have passed, when someone says Umar, first comes to mind "justice."

THE GOVERNOR THAT WAS CALLED TO ACCOUNT

T he Caliph Umar divided the state into administrative units and assigned a governor for each administrative region. He divided the regions into provinces, districts, and small towns. He paid a great attention to the administration of these places and acted meticulously in choosing and controlling the governors and other officials. During each hajj period, he used to stand before the governors with the people for whom they served and ask people whether they were content with their governors or not.

During one of those hajj periods, he gathered the governors and listened to the complaints of people. People also offered their views of their governors. One man wanted to speak and in a rather shy manner said:

"That governor of yours unjustly gave me a hundred beatings."

At that moment, a deep silence fell and everybody was surprised and waiting to see what would happen. Some started to talk among themselves in this way:

"While sending his governors to the administrative units, the caliph sent out letters to the people saying that 'As long as your governor acts fairly, you shall obey his commands. If he does not act justly, immediately let me know.' We will see whether he will find a solution as he says."

While they were talking in this way, the caliph turned to the man about whom that person complained and asked, "Is that all that man said right? Did you beat that man?" "Yes, I did," he replied. The caliph further asked, "Then, can you explain the reasonable grounds for beating that man?"

The governor could not come up with a valid reason.

Everyone was in silence and waiting what would happen next. Umar addressed the man that was complaining and said:

"With what did the governor beat you?"

"With a whip."

"You take this whip. Do the same in front of us."

Most of the people there had not guessed that Umar would decide on such a thing. However, Amr ibn al-As, who was one of the governors himself, had already predicted the decision of Umar. Because as a governor, Amr knew very well that Umar was rather sensitive on such issues. He asked to speak and said:

"O Chief of Believers! You should not do this. If you do such a thing in front of people, the influence of the governors over people will be diminished, and they will not be able to serve well.

These words did not change the decision of the caliph. He addressed the governors waiting there:

"Did I not explain to you and warn all of you during your appointment of the following: 'I am not appointing you to dominate or put pressure on the people. You will be a guide of truth for them. Preserve all the rights of the Muslims. Always stay in contact with them so that the powerful do not oppress the powerless. Do not regard yourself as superior to any other Muslim.'"

The governors replied:

"Yes, you warned all of us in this way."

The caliph stopped for a moment. Then he told the complaining one:

"Come and do the same."

Understanding that Umar would back down from his decision, Amr said:

"If we persuade the plaintiff, will you cancel the punishment?"

"If the plaintiff agrees, it is okay. If not, the governor will be punished."

Amr went to the plaintiff and tried to persuade him to withdraw his complaint.

At last, Amr persuaded the plaintiff on the condition that he would receive one gold piece in lieu of each beating. In this way, the governor was saved from being beat. This event heavily influenced both the people and the public servants on duty. From that day on, the public servants attached much more importance to their attitudes and acts while they were on duty. The people also saw that their rights were well protected and thus felt more secure.

THE PRIEST THAT MADE
THE CALIPH CRY

U mar, together with several Companions,
were passing in front of a monastery and
saw a priest with a white beard and a head
of pure, white hair. All of sudden something
happened to the caliph. He sat on the ground
and started to cry. The Companions were very
surprised and asked each other:

"What happened?"

Yet none of them found an answer to this
question. One of them asked Umar:

"O Chief of Believers, what made you cry so
much?"

Umar, pointing at the priest in the monastery, said:

"He is almost at the end of his life. Unfortunately, however, he was not able to know the

Messenger of God, who came for the salvation of people and was unable to be included in community. I am crying for that old person."

Umar was crying for the person whom he never knew before and who could not find truth.

IN THE NAME OF THAT LOVE

U mar established certain organizations that were dealt with the issues of crime and safety, controlling the sellers and regulating the daily relations of people, and he put everybody—women, men, slaves or free persons—on a certain stipend.

That month the stipends were being distributed as usual and everybody was waiting for their turn. Usama, the son of Zayd, who was the foster child of the Messenger of God, approached the distribution site and received his share. Some of the Companions saw the amount of Usama's stipend. Among these was the son of Umar, Abdullah.

Then it was Abdullah's turn to receive his stipend. The official presented Abdullah his stipend as well. Receiving his share, Abdullah realized that his stipend was a bit less than that of Usama. Coming closer to the official who was distributing the salaries, he asked:

"Did you make a mistake in calculating the amount of my stipend?"

Upon this, the official looked at the list again and the amount that Abdullah received. Turning to Abdullah, he said:

"No, sir there is no mistake. I also asked the other officials; your father decided on this amount for your stipend."

In fact, Abdullah was not jealous of the stipend Usama received. He was only thinking that he should also receive the same amount of stipend. That evening, he asked his father, the Caliph Umar in a shy manner:

"My dear father, today, during the distribution of the stipends, I saw that the stipend of Usama, the son of Zayd, was more than mine. What is it that makes Usama superior to me or that makes me lacking? Why is his share more than mine?"

Umar answered his son's question in this way:

"My son, I cannot know the thing that makes him superior to you or that makes you lacking. However, there is something I know. It is the fact that the Messenger of God loved his father more than your father and loved Usama more than you. I too, in the name of that love, see Usama superior to you."

Anything the Messenger of God regarded important was highly valuable for him. When he needed to make a preference, he would put into practice the preferences of the Messenger of God even to the disadvantage of his own son.

THE DRAIN THAT DROPS BLOOD

I t was Friday. It was almost time for Friday prayers. Umar went out of his house and was thinking about the sermon that he was going to deliver for the Friday prayer. While he was passing right in front of the house of Abbas, the uncle of the Messenger of God, he saw several drops of blood on his clothes. When he looked at the direction the drops were falling, he saw that they were falling from a drain on the roof. The caliph, who focused on the sermon he would deliver, was annoyed.

He murmured "Who is it that is killing an animal on that roof and making my clothing dirty? Later, in that mood, he reached the drain and knocked it down. In those dirty clothes, he could not go to the Masjid and perform the

Friday prayer. He turned back to his house. He changed his clothes. Then he came to the Masjid. He went on the *minbar* to deliver the sermon. He explained what he had planned before. In general, at the end of his sermon he would allocate a time for the solution of the problems of the Muslims. That day, the topic was the event he experienced at that day. According to Umar, that event was not something personal. It could have happened to anyone else as well. In order to warn people, he said:

"O people! Think well about the consequences of the things you perform for others. While coming to the Masjid, I was passing in front of a house. Drops of blood fell on me from a drain on the roof. I hit that drain and knocked it down."

It was only seconds after Umar finished his words that Abbas shouted:

"O Umar, what did you do? What did you do?"

Abbas understood right away that it was his drain since he knew Umar passed in front of his house on his way to the Masjid.

However, Umar could not understand this reaction of Abbas. For this reason, he explained:

"It could have caused big problems for the other people as well. That's why, I hit and knocked it down."

Umar was going to go on speaking when Abbas stood up and said:

"O Umar what did you do? I saw it myself that that drain was put there by the Messenger of God."

This was enough for Umar to fall on the ground. Umar, who bore a great respect for anything related to God's Messenger, would not have even touched at that drain if he had known that it was touched by the Prophet let alone put there by himself.

Some time later, Umar regained his consciousness. He slowly stood up. Looking at Abbas he said:

"I will put my head at the bottom of that wall and you, by setting your feet on my head, will put that drain in its place. Until you put that drain in its place, I will not raise my head."

Then, as a result of Umar's insistence on this, Abbas promised to do so. They immediately went to the house of Abbas after the Friday prayer. Umar, as he said in the Masjid, put his head at the bottom of the wall. Abbas could do nothing else. Was it easy to make Umar give up his idea when he was so decisive about something? Abbas stood on the head of Umar and put the drain in its place where the Messenger of God had first put it. Umar was now in peace because the memory of the noble Prophet would live. They put the drain in its original place but decided not to butcher an animal on the roof from that day on so that no blood dropped from the drain. They could not let people be disturbed by this. If the Messenger of God had also seen that it was causing trouble for people, he would have also pulled that drain from the roof. However, the Companions who were longing for him, could never touch that drain upon learning the reality.

FOR THE SAKE OF THE TRUE TRANSFER OF HIS WORDS

U mar, being among the prominent one among the Companions in all fields, was also among those who knew best the *hadiths* of the Messenger of God. He was very meticulous in relating the *hadiths*. One day when he was at his home, one of the leading names of the Companions, Abu Musa al-Ashari came to visit him. He knocked at the door three times. At that moment, Umar was busy doing something so he was a bit late in opening the door. After knocking at the door three times, the door was not opened so Abu Musa al-Ashari decided to leave. He had only taken a few steps back when Umar finished his work and told those at home:

"I heard Abu Musa. Open the door."

Then the one who opened the door said:

"There is nobody at the door; he is gone."

Umar said in wonder:

"Abu Musa must have understood that I was busy. Why did he leave?"

Then, he instructed the person who was with him:

"Go and find him. Tell him to come to me."

That person walked a bit and found Abu Musa. After saying, "Peace be with you," he added:

"The Chief of Believers is waiting for you."

Abu Musa immediately turned around and came to the house of Umar.

Umar asked him:

"O Abu Musa, I had something to do when you came. Then we looked only to see that you had left. Why didn't you wait?"

Abu Musa answered this question:

"O Caliph of the Messenger of God! The Prophet ordered us, 'When you go to someone's home, knock at the door three times and ask for permission to enter. If there is no permission, then turn back.'"

Umar hadn't heard such a *hadith* from God's Messenger. Nevertheless, Prophet Muhammad, peace and blessings be upon him, could have said this. Even though Umar was one of the closest Companions to the Messenger of God, he had not always been with him during the day. Thus, it was very natural for him not to know some of his *hadith*s. However, Umar was still uneasy about this. He wanted to know for sure whether this *hadith* was correct or not as he wanted to transfer everything of the Messenger of God in the correct way to the upcoming generations. Abu Musa was one of his closest friends, yet he wanted to be completely sure about the origin of this *hadith*. Turning to his friend, he said:

"O Abu Musa, I haven't heard this *hadith*. You should bring evidence showing that this belongs to the Messenger of God."

Abu Musa had heard this *hadith* many years ago. So, how could he find evidence now? The best way was to find someone who had been among the listeners when God's Messenger explained this *hadith*. It had been a long time, and he had already forgotten who were there at that time. Yet he could not say this to Umar since he knew that Umar would never accept such evidence. He left Umar. He directly went to the Masjid. He knew that there was always someone there at any hour of the day, either praying or talking. Seeing Abu Musa worried, the people there asked:

"What is wrong Abu Musa? Why are you so worried?"

Abu Musa explained what had happened. Then he asked:

"Is there anyone else who heard this *hadith*?"

It was Ubay ibn Ka'b that relieved Abu Musa:

"It is not only the old people that had heard this *hadith* but also the younger ones."

Then pointing at Abu Said al-Khudri, he said, "Take Abu Said to Umar."

Abu Musa was rather relieved now. He didn't want to lose any time. Together with Abu Said, he came to Umar. They knocked at the door. The moment they entered inside, Abu Musa said:

"O Chief of Believers! There are some people other than me that heard this *hadith* from the Messenger of God. Here is Abu Said. He is one of them."

Umar was convinced now. Turning to Abu Musa, he said:

"O Abu Musa, I didn't accuse you of something. The only thing I wanted was to ensure that people did not attribute something that was not true to God's Messenger."

Both Abu Musa and Abu Said found the justification of Umar right. Saying farewell, they left the caliph.

WHAT WAS IT THAT MADE UMAR CRY AND SMILE

There were two things that deeply influenced Umar. When he remembered one of these, Umar would lose himself and weep loudly. On the contrary, when he remembered the other, he would smile. The thing that made the Caliph Umar cry was the fact that Umar had buried his little daughter alive in the pre-Islamic era of paganism. Anytime he remembered this, it was as if he aged one year. No matter where he was, his voice would go hoarse and tears would run down his beard. At such a moment he would say to himself: "O Umar, how could you do such a thing?"

The thing that made Umar laugh was the idols he had made before Islam. They had made some of these idols from *halva* and then worshiped them. When they felt hungry, they had eaten these idols. Whenever the caliph remembered this event, he would think how funny it was and laugh at it.

A DESIRE THAT NEVER
FADED AWAY ALL HIS LIFE

One day when Umar was on the *minbar* for the sermon. He talked about Adn, which was one of the highest stations in Paradise. People were excited, looking at the caliph and listening to his words. Umar first said that this place would be so large and its doors so big alike. Then he talked about some other features of this station in Paradise. Then he added:

"It is the Prophets who will first enter this station of Paradise."

Pointing to the holy grave of the Messenger of God, he said:

"How happy the owner of that grave."

People were listening to Umar in wonder while Umar went on explaining:

"After the Prophets come the truthful ones."

Pointing to the grave of Abu Bakr, who was the loyal friend of the Messenger of God, he said:

"How happy the owner of that grave."

Umar went on and the Companions were curious to hear who was next.

"Then people who died in the name of God will enter into this station Paradise."

After this word, he did not add something else. He went deep into thought. Maybe he remembered the news the Messenger of God said that he would be among these people. He heard this good news, but he still felt the fear of not being among those people. Deep in these thoughts, he murmured: "How could you be one of those who died in the name of God? Do you deserve such a thing?"

The Companions were waiting for Umar, and he said this prayer for him:

"I hope God, Who granted you with Islam, with the Migration, and made you the friend of the Prophet and again Who provided you with the chance of living in Medina, will grant you the realization of your desire to die for the sake of Him as well."

DAGGER WOUND

I t was one of those days when Umar went to the bazaar for the inspection. He approached those trading and asked them whether or not they had any problems. Those undergoing any problem came to him and shared their problem with him, and he sought solutions to their problems. While he was talking with someone, he realized there was someone else waiting for him. After solving his problem, he approached the person who was waiting there. This person was Abu Lulu, who was the slave of Mughera ibn Shuba. He had not accepted Islam. However, Umar exerted great to solve the people's problems regardless if they were Muslim. The caliph thought of it in this way: "If a sheep is caught by a wolf at the side of the Euphrates, God will ask me about this." In a calm manner and smiling, he turned to this slave and said:

"Let me know your problem."

"Mughera burdened me with a heavy tax."

"What are you dealing with? How much do you earn?"

Lulu said:

"I am a carpenter, blacksmith, and embroiderer."

"They told me that someone made a windmill, is it you?"

"Yes, I can build very strong windmills."

"Then you must be earning well from these professions. The tax you pay to Mughera must not be too much for you."

Abu Lulu did not get the support he was expecting from Umar. He felt bad and wanted to immediately leave that place. Umar said:

"Can you build a windmill for me in return for money?"

"Of course, I can. I will build a windmill for you that will be talked by everyone both in the east and in the west."

Umar was not aware that it was by the hand of this slave that he would die in the name of

God. Abu Lulu had long before decided to stab Umar with a dagger.

It had not even been twenty hours since the conversation between Umar and Abu Lulu in the market. The caliph woke up to perform his night prayer. He performed an ablution. He started to pray. Deepening into the meaning of prayer, he lost himself as usual. He always performed his prayers in a great awe. He couldn't stop crying in most of his prayers in the Masjid. After performing prayer, he went to bed again and rested a bit.

Then, he got up to get ready for morning prayer. He performed an ablution and changed his clothes. He headed towards the Masjid to lead the prayer. The Companions were also coming to the Masjid one by one in order to perform prayer in a congregation. The streets were crowded as if it had been noon. Among this crowd there was one person whose intention was totally different than the others. That person was Abu Lulu. While all the people were going to the Masjid for the sake of God, Abu Lulu was present for his bad intentions.

Umar entered the first line as the imam while the other people took the back rows. Abu Lulu entered the line that was close to Umar. The caliph lifted his hands up and started to lead the prayer by saying *"Allahu Akbar."* The congregation did the same. Abu Lulu, who was not Muslim, pretended to pray in order not to appear different from the other people. Then they altogether bowed their heads. Abu Lulu found it very hard to bow his head because of the dagger he was carrying. Then first Umar followed by the other Companions prostrated themselves in prayer.

Abu Lulu said to himself, "This is the time," and took the dagger he was hiding and thrust it into Umar. With that grudge, he thrust Umar with the dagger six times. The last dagger stroke went into the lower belly of Umar, and this strike made Umar fall down. Everyone was shocked by this and did not know what to do.

Umar, in the meantime, asked about the person who stabbed him with a dagger because it was very important for the big caliph, the best exemplary of justice. He had never done any injustice to anyone. He thought, "Umar, to whom did you do an injustice?" That was not possible, of course. Could the one who spent anything of himself for others have done such a thing? When the Companions said it was an unbelieving slave, Umar said:

"Thanks to God that I was not killed by someone who believed in God and performed his prayer."

Umar was not aware of the severity of the stabbing so he tried to sit up. But he couldn't. He fell down again. He was bleeding so much, and in that state he was carried to his house by the Companions. He was half awake. They couldn't bring his consciousness back. Those who were very close to him knew what would open his eyes if he did not die. One of these people said:

"If he is still alive, you can wake him up only by saying "O Umar, it is time for prayer."

He was right. One of them said:

"O Chief of Believers! It is time for prayer. This time, saying 'Anyone not performing prayer will not be able to benefit from Islam,' which he had reiterated many times in his life, Umar sat up and tried to stand up."

However, especially because of that big stabbing into his lower belly, he couldn't. Seeing that Umar was still alive, the Companions were very happy. They did not leave him even for a minute and all were working for his treatment. Days passed, yet there was no progress in the state of Umar. He could neither eat nor drink. When the Companions that was serving him said:

"O Umar, do you want something to eat?"

He couldn't find the strength to speak and only said "No" by his eyes.

However, when the same Companions said: "O Umar, time for prayer," he immediately sat up and said: "My prayer." He was performing his prayer even while drops of blood were falling from his body. It was because he had seen the utmost importance the Messenger of God, whom he loved so much, had attached to prayer.

Again, days passed, but there was no progress in Umar's condition. To the contrary, his situation was deteriorating. Everyone was aware that Umar would never recover. The idea that the Muslims would have no leader was not possible, of course. One day, some of the Companions went to visit him and asked:

"Can you suggest someone as the leader of the Muslims after you?"

Umar went into deep thought. Then he said:

"If I appoint someone for my position after me, you should know that the one who was more beneficial than me did the same. If I do not appoint someone as such, you should also know that the one who was more beneficial than me did the same."

With these words, Umar was implying the Messenger of God, who had not appointed someone to govern the dominion after himself and Abu Bakr, who had appointed him to govern the dominion. Umar had always taken these two people as his model. Hours were passing and the Companions waited to hear a name from Umar. Umar was both trying to cope with his pains and thinking about this problem of the Muslims. He did not want the Muslims to be leaderless after him. He knew that there would appear some dissidence on this matter. Turning to people there he said:

"If Abu Ubayda had lived, I would have chosen him. If God had asked the reason why I chose him, I would have said the words of the

Messenger of God: 'It is Abu Ubayda who is the most reliable one among the Muslims.'"

However, Abu Ubayda was not alive. Umar went on speaking although it was very hard to do. People there were trying to hear him. He said:

"If Salim, the slave of Abu Hudhayfa, had been alive, I would have chosen him. If God had asked the reason why I chose him, I would have said that I had heard the Messenger of God saying: 'It is Salim who loves God most.'"

When one of those people suggested:

"What if your son, Abdullah comes after you?"

He said:

"No, he cannot execute this mission."

When the people went on asking the name of the one who would govern the land, he said:

"My purpose here is to choose the one that is most appropriate and will govern you best. I am putting all of my efforts to this end."

He closed his eyes and went into deep thoughts. Then he opened his eyes and addressed people there:

"Ali ibn Abu Talib, Uthman ibn Affan, Abdurrahman ibn Awf, Sa'd ibn Abi Waqqas,

Zubayr ibn Awwam, and Talha ibn Ubaydul-
lah... These people all gather at somewhere and
decide on someone as the caliph."

The names Umar uttered were among the
people who had been promised Paradise. Umar
wanted the caliph that would follow him to be
one of these names.

He assigned his son as the arbiter for these
people so that they could work well. He had one
more desire on this issue. He expressed his wish
in this way:

"This should be handled immediately. The
solution should be found before my body is buried."

Umar who spent everything of himself in the
name of God maintained his life with the salary given to him during his caliphate. However,
he did not spend all of this salary, but instead
he used it for the sake of God. He borrowed
money for his family and did not want to be late
in paying back. Now he was in his bed stabbed
with the dagger of an unbeliever and living his
last days. Because he could not stand up, he
couldn't pay his loans. Yet he was aware of his
debt. He wanted to deal with this without losing

any time. He called his son Abdullah and told him:

"My son, calculate the total of our debt."

Abdullah came later and said:

"It is 86 thousand dirhams."

"My son, go and pay this money with the properties that belong to my family. If it does not suffice, request the rest from the sons of Adiyy ibn Ka'b. If that does not suffice either, then request the rest from the Quraysh tribe. Be sure that we do not owe to anyone."

Upon this request of his father, Abdullah went and sold their properties in order to pay back all of their debts.

THE LAST DESIRE

Even though Umar was on his deathbed, he was still dealing with important matters. However, in the last days his pains got much worse. He could neither get up nor speak anymore. He had a last desire: to be able to be close to the Messenger of God and his loyal friend Abu Bakr with whom he was always together both spiritually and physically.

Umar, after accepting Islam, had always been together with the Messenger of God regardless of his work. He could not go even a few days without seeing him. The deaths of God's Messenger and his loyal friend Abu Bakr had deeply affected Umar, and he could not bear being away from them anymore. Since he had never been away from these two friends in his life, he did not want to leave them after his death as well. So he needed to take the permission of Aisha, who was the closest to these two people; she was the wife of the Messenger of God and the daughter of Abu Bakr.

Umar told his son Abdullah:

"My son, go to the mother of the Muslims, Aisha. Convey my greetings to her, and tell her: 'Umar asks for your permission to be buried next to his two friends.' Nevertheless, never tell her that 'The Chief of Believers wishes it to be so' because I am no longer the caliph."

Now, he was experiencing his very last moments. Sometimes he was fainted and later came to himself. He found it very hard to breathe now. Abdullah, without losing any time, went to the mother of the Muslims, Aisha. He conveyed the greetings of his father. It was very difficult for Aisha to make such a decision as she had thought of this place for herself before. She also did not want to reject the last desire of the great Caliph Umar, who spent everything of himself in the name of God and who loved the Messenger of God and Abu Bakr so much. She was one of those who knew very well his devotion to the Messenger of God and Abu Bakr. Considering the issue from this perspective, Aisha told Abdullah:

"I had thought of that place for myself before. However, if the Chief of Believers desires it, I cannot say no to him. He can be buried there."

Abdullah, in a big joy, left Aisha. He wanted to let his father, who was lying on his deathbed, know this happy news. He knew very well how important this message was for his father.

Umar was wondering what Aisha's answer would be. How couldn't he think about it? Each day, his desire to reach his friends was growing more and more, and he was dying for this. Therefore, he stared at the door waiting to see his son coming with good news. Abdullah returned and even before Umar asked about the result, he said:

"I've got good news, father! Aisha accepted your will. You will be buried next to the Messenger of God and Abu Bakr."

This made Umar very happy. His eyes which had not looked happy for days were full of happiness now, and his face which had gone pale was now smiling. His biggest desire had been accepted. Those who could not understand Umar's state even thought that he was recovering.

Umar was very happy with this news, yet he had some fear in himself as well. He could not stop thinking, "What if Aisha changes her mind." He knew how important this place was for her as well. He transferred his concern to the people there in this way:

"When I die, take and bury me in the grave that is next to those of the Messenger of God and Abu Bakr. Ask again Aisha for permission. If she permits, bury me there. If she changes her mind and does not permit it, then bury me in the graveyard where the vast majority of the Muslims are buried."

Soon after this speech of the caliph, he reached his Creator after a caliphate of ten years and six months, in the 23rd year of the Migration. God accepted his prayer to die in the name of God. After his death, as he said in his will, he was buried next to the grave of the Messenger of God. Aisha, the mother of the Muslims, was asked again for her permission. Complying with her earlier decision, she permitted him to be buried there. Thus, Umar, who had not been spiritually away from his friends even for a minute, was also with them physically. None of the three had differed from each other in the years they lived as well. As a result of the will of God, they each had died at the age of 63. May God grant us the privilege to be their neighbors in the Hereafter.